"Hey! Don't Shoot, I'm The Guitar Man! I should have known that Buzzy Martin, the author of this unique book, would have had a wonderful story to tell. This is such a mesmerizing book, you feel like you're in prison along with Buzzy's students. I certainly recommend this book, not only to musicians, but also to families who might have at-risk youth or loved ones who are incarcerated. Eventually, this retrospective of a music program in a prison setting will become a block buster film and then, there will be many more people moved, because of Buzzy's work giving so much of his time and helping the less fortunate, all through the spirit of his music."

— Hal Blaine, World's Most Recorded Musician
Member of the Rock and Roll Hall of Fame
Member of Nashville Musician's Hall of Fame

"After twenty-seven years of working in San Quentin, a person no longer finds the perspective or view that is offered in Buzzy's piece. I thank him for pulling a string, and finding a note in me that I thought was busted and had long gone dead."

— Len Carl, Correctional Officer Retired

"Buzzy's book captures the mood and specter of the novitiate's introduction to the world inside prison walls. What he finds, learns, and shares is the common humanity that still exists in spite of it all. As one who has spent his career in the criminal justice system, I can vouch for its authenticity and also the novel journey it took me on."

— Elliot Daum, Superior Court Judge

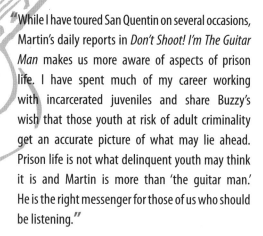

"My two trips to San Quentin State Prison for parole hearings did not allow me to obtain nearly the depth of knowledge Buzzy's repeated trips inside the facility afforded him. It did, however, provide me enough information to know that this book reveals the truth about life inside the Q. His stark description of prison life, and the impact on prisoners' lives, is chilling in its honesty."

— Jeff Weaver, Chief of Police

"While I have toured San Quentin on several occasions, Martin's daily reports in *Don't Shoot! I'm The Guitar Man* makes us more aware of aspects of prison life. I have spent much of my career working with incarcerated juveniles and share Buzzy's wish that those youth at risk of adult criminality get an accurate picture of what may lie ahead. Prison life is not what delinquent youth may think it is and Martin is more than 'the guitar man.' He is the right messenger for those of us who should be listening."

— Robert G. Gillen, Chief Probation Officer Retired

"*Don't Shoot, I'm the Guitar Man* is a riveting compilation of Buzzy Martin's experiences teaching music at San Quentin Prison. He graphically describes the despair that a prison environment spawns, truly a place no young person would like to inhabit, much less aspire to. This book is a must-read for everyone, but especially for parents and young people who could potentially become emeshed in this nightmare. Read what he has to say. It is simple and profound."

— Bill Roventini, City of Sebastopol Councilman, retired

"It has been my pleasure to read Buzzy Martin's *Don't Shoot! I'm The Guitar Man*. I am a teacher who works with at-risk youth incarcerated in Juvenile Hall. The kids I work with are involved in gangs, drugs, violence, and the court system. Though the work is rewarding, it is at most times difficult at best. I am continually looking for reading materials that my students can learn from. I would highly encourage all at-risk students to read this book. It does not preach nor attempt to scare but tells the story of one man's experience teaching a music program to inmates locked up behind the walls of San Quentin Prison. The language is not difficult, the concept important, and the journey you are taken on through the words of Buzzy Martin makes for an emotional impact on the reader."

— Celia Lamantia, MA Education, Juvenile Hall Teacher

"It was with great interest that I read *Don't Shoot! I'm The Guitar Man* by Buzzy Martin. His book immediately captured my attention and held it to the last page. His writing is vivid and descriptive, creating a vision of life within San Quentin Prison that still haunts me to this day. I was especially touched by his message to young people in trouble that they should not fall into the trap of believing being sentenced to San Quentin is somehow a badge of honor. It is a brutal place where all honor is destroyed and everyone falls victim to the lowest depths of degradation. I hope those who read his book would come to understand how severe the penalties of incarceration truly are, and anyone who believes living in the 'Q' is acceptable will quickly change their minds."

— Robert Tavonatti, Principal, Court School and Juvenile Hall

I met Buzzy Martin fourteen years ago. I was the sergeant with the Petaluma Police Department and had been assigned the duties of Press Information Officer during the Polly Klaas kidnapping investigation. Buzzy had written and recorded a song to raise money to help find Polly. I would see Buzzy at different events through the years and heard of his work with kids at risk in our community and locked up at juvenile hall. After my election as a county supervisor in 1998, I went to see Buzzy's music program in juvenile hall. I was struck by how easily Buzzy communicated with the boys and girls about the importance of education and staying out of trouble all the while teaching them about music.

Don't Shoot! I'm The Guitar Man is a raw emotional account of Buzzy's hours teaching music to inmates in San Quentin Prison. Parts of his book made me laugh while others had me crying. His stories paint a picture of life in a prison that most of us will never experience. Buzzy's book is a valuable tool and a must read for all juvenile hall kids or anyone with an at-risk youth who may be headed for the wrong side of the law. If one kid reads this book and decides prison life is not for him, then Buzzy has succeeded in his journey.

When I set out to write this, I was concerned that my friendship with Buzzy might compromise the credibility of my statement. Instead, it's truly strengthened my respect and admiration for him. My friend, you are a very special, brave, and caring person. Thank you for sharing your stories with all of us and helping us understand the precious value of the word freedom.

— Sonoma County Supervisor Mike Kerns

DON'T SHOOT!

I'm the Guitar Man

Buzzy Martin

Buzzard Press • Sebastopol • 2007

Cover illustration by Stacy Meinzen
Book design by Jo-Anne Rosen

ISBN: 978-0-9793508-0-1

First Printing

Printed in China through
Global Interprint, Santa Rosa, California

Buzzard Press
Sebastopol, California

Acknowledgments

I would like to thank Carol Lundberg, Jo-Anne Rosen, and Lorna Johnson for their professional critique. They have been a tremendous help and have always believed in this project.

Thanks to Bill Roventini and Leonard Carl for their suggestions during the refinement stages, as well as the many people, too numerous to mention by name, who offered their feedback and encouragement.

I am especially grateful to my wife and son, Laura and Casey, for loving me and for being the very first ones to suggest that I write this book.

A big thank you to Jane Flood, Charles "Smitty" Golczynski, and Sean Cuccaro for loving me and believing in me.

My thanks to Georgeanne Rice for all of her time typing this book from a handwritten manuscript to the computer, to Kathy Allen for all of the hours of listening to the prison stories over the cell phone, to Stacy Meinzen of Graphics in Green for bringing my idea of a cover illustration to fruition and to Jo-Anne Rosen for editing and layout services.

And of course, I would like to thank all of my inmate music students, prison staff and both the inmates and the officers of San Quentin State Prison who made me very aware of the things that most people could barely perceive.

To My Parents

Harold and Marie

Contents

DON'T SHOOT!

I'm the Guitar Man

Introduction

"What's a guy like me doing
in a place like this?"

"You want me to teach music in prison? Are you nuts?" That was my first thought when it was suggested I teach a music program at San Quentin State Prison. If someone had told me a few years ago I would be teaching music at one of the most famous prisons in the United States, instead of playing in night clubs, I think I would have laughed until my face fell off. This is my story, my road trip teaching music in a prison setting. There are some funny stories and a lot of sad ones. Sort of a journey to hell and back with a tear in my eye and a smile on my face.

I was born and raised in Grand Rapids, Michigan and began playing music pretty early in life. I started out with high school dances and backyard parties. After high school came bar gigs. Lots of them. I must have played every beer joint in western Michigan before I reached twenty-one. In the summer of 1979 I had a chance to move to Northern California and I took it without ever looking back. As a singer-guitar player who writes all his own songs, my number one goal was to try and get a record contract. But like millions of other musicians who came to California in 1979 seeking fame and fortune, I never landed the big record deal. What did happen was I met a great lady, we got married, had a child and started a family. I still play music every day, I still write songs, and my life could not have turned out any better.

I also teach music to at-risk kids, or as some people call them, "throwaway children." I didn't know it at the time, but the road leading to my work at San Quentin began when a family friend

1

in the fall of 1996 asked if I would be interested in teaching music to kids who have been in trouble with the law. She told me it could be as little as one hour a week and she would pay me $50.00 for my time.

My first thought was no way! I have enough things going on in my life to keep me busy for a long time, but I could really use that $50.00 a week. So after thinking it over for a few days, I decided to take this project on. And as they say, the rest is history. Within a year I went from one class per day every week to teaching eighteen classes a week.

Eight years later I'm teaching music at Juvenile Halls, Clean and Sober High Schools, group homes and Probation Camps for Boys. I see a lot of abused boys, girls, and kids in gangs as young as twelve years old.

As word spread about these music classes and how good they made the kids feel, I received a phone call from one of the teachers at Juvenile Hall asking me if I would be interested in teaching a music class at San Quentin State Prison. She went on to say that her best friend oversees the art program at San Quentin and would love to have me teach music to the inmates. After talking it over with my wife, I decided to give it a try. My feeling has always been to live life to its fullest and be as open minded as possible.

I signed a contract for twelve weeks at the Q, not realizing I would end up teaching music there for three and a half years. I have found that using music as a tool to teach troubled teens and inmates in prison really works. Music does heal the soul. It seems to reopen a place of innocence and joy that bypasses even the most troubled personal history. For two hours each week, guilt, shame, fear and abuse can be forgotten. At the very least, the frustration and rage that create prison problems are lessened. At best, something in these men that has been on the verge of dying is preserved and renewed so that when they are free they have something positive to sustain them.

Music for Kids At Risk

The Music for Kids-At-Risk program I created brings a musical experience to a targeted population of children often called throwaway kids. I go to classrooms in correctional and protective custody facilities, court and community alternative schools and special education pre-schools and teach them how to play and sing the music they love. I have watched rival gang members who have never spoken to each other inside these facilities, and who would be fighting each other on the streets, playing together and supporting each other through the music. With this program, music provides the communicative link to others. It has proved beneficial to many children.

One of the biggest reasons I decided to take on the job at San Quentin Prison was because of the young and up-and-coming gang bangers who were starting to pop up in Juvenile Hall. Every one of these kids loves hard-core rap music and embraces the whole gangster lifestyle. Boys and girls alike. I felt that by working with real-life inmates as a music teacher I could share with these kids what I learned about the grim, unglamorized life at San Quentin, and give them an accurate picture of their futures if they do not make some major changes in their lives.

Kids are resilient, but they need exposure to positive and creative social activity. If these "at risk" children who are part of the juvenile justice system and otherwise underprivileged are going to have a chance to live a decent life and not be a constant drain on the community, then programs like this are a key ingredient. Music empowers kids and gives them the gift of self-discovery.

The class consists of a combination of music history and appreciation, highlighted by demonstrations of different musical instruments and topped off with the student's participation. While making music, the kids discover a deeper sense of discipline and accomplishment.

These teens are also in need of positive adult role models, adults who care about them. I believe every child deserves to be a kid even though most of the students that I work with have failed in comprehensive schools, engaged in illegal activities, are possible rival gang members and usually support each other in negative and destructive behaviors. Their lives are centered around destruction.

What I bring to these kids is a great opportunity to experience risk taking and the power of creation all through the magic of music. I'm committed to these students. I feel that with music in their hearts they can be a valuable asset to their communities and themselves. The one thing you can't ever forget is they are just kids. To see self-described street thugs joining together to sing a song is truly an incredible sight. The bottom line is this music program helps kids learn to become kids.

My hope was that by extending my music programs to San Quentin, I would not only be helping the inmates, but also be acquiring real-life experience about the horror of prison life to motivate my at-risk kids to change.

Inside San Quentin

What is it like inside the Q? It is like visiting another country and best undertaken with a guide. For readers undertaking this journey with me, the following describes the levels of incarceration, organization, facilities, and some of the terminology used at San Quentin.

Inmate Point System: Levels of Incarceration

The State of California in 1972 devised a system for determining levels of incarceration. The 1971 riot in Attica Prison in New York State was analyzed and some objective criteria developed to predict measures of an inmate's behavior. They came up with a scoring system based on twenty-six elements, including the crime, age of criminal, age at first offense, etc..

Level 1 – Scored between 0-18, which, in the prison business, is called lightweight felons. These inmates have minimum security. They can go to the Ranch; they have the least amount of time to serve, and not a lot of violence or personal violence within their historical background.

Level 2 – Scored between 19-37. These inmates have a little bit more time to serve or some other factors that are more serious that cause the housing to be done in a more secure location. San Quentin is mostly Level 2.

Level 3 – Scored between 38-51. These inmates have even more serious case elements in their background.

Level 4 – Scored between 52 and above. There are some inmates with points as high as 960. Some inmates just can't stop misbehaving and every time they do they get a disciplinary and every disciplinary adds more points to their record, to their level. An inmate who's a Level 1 who's got 17-18 points could receive a lot of 115's or disciplinary actions; the more infractions that he receives for serious rule violations, the more points are added on. So a pretty easygoing fellow gets a drunk driving conviction and winds up in front of a judge and the judge sentences him to a year and a day or more and he comes to state prison. Then if he continues to misbehave, by getting into trouble or disrupting the program, he can earn his points in a negative way and wind up in a higher security setting, up to a Level 4. Pelican Bay, Folsom, and Sacramento State Prison are all Level 4 prisons and San Quentin was until 1989; now it's a Level 2.

Units In San Quentin Prison

There are five units in San Quentin Prison and five ways to divide up the prison. There are also five housing units within the prison and each unit has an assigned associate warden. H-Unit is Unit 5 but that includes the Ranch as well. Unit 1 is North Block, the Adjustment Center and Death Row. South Block is a unit and the Reception Center is a unit.

Adjustment Center (Security Housing Unit)

I would tell people that the Adjustment Center is not the end of the world, but you can see it from there. It's a prison within a prison. Inmates are separated from society because of the stuff they did. While they're in prison some inmates continue to do bad things and they can't be allowed to remain in the general population. So they're separated and isolated in the Adjustment Center. It's a single cell, totally locked down environment. Inmates are handcuffed any time they're outside of their cells. They're strip searched constantly. It's the baddest of the bad. It's the worst guys in the penal system.

The Adjustment Center was built in 1959 when rehabilitation was an up-and-coming thing in America. It was set up so that there was either a social worker, psychiatrist, psychologist, and one officer on site. Within the Adjustment Center are a few large rooms that were used for group therapy. The elements that changed it are numerous and took years. Eventually, the rehabilitative model was washed away and gradually the Adjustment Center became a punitive place. Originally inmates freely roamed the Adjustment Center. They would cook their own meals and have group therapy, but over time that faded away and it became the last place on earth.

It's now called "Security Housing Unit." It is the end of the line within the prison system. The good people of California built Pelican Bay Prison and moved the Level 4 inmates that were housed in the Adjustment Center up there.

H-Unit

H-Unit has double fencing, barbwire on all sides, gun coverage all the way around. That partly defines what a Level 2 is. H-Unit houses Level 2 and some Level 3 inmates. In H-Unit inmates are expected to work because of various operations in San Quentin — for example there's a Reception Center in San Quentin for Northern California. Those are the inmates in orange jumpsuits. It has grown a lot in the last few years so it's taking more and more bed cells up in San Quentin.

North Block (The Hill)

These inmates are the lifers. These guys might have very low points but they're in for the rest of their life. They work in the prison industry. They're good workers. Prison jobs consist of making furniture, maintenance, plumbing, electric, and maintaining the machines that run the laundry. The buildings are named based upon the orientation of north, south, east, and west.

The Ranch (Level 1)

The Ranch is a minimum level security facility, no 18-foot fences just 3-foot fences. It's based upon the inmates' level of behavior, and their potentiality as determined by objective standards as was mentioned on their score sheets. If an inmate has to serve any more than a year, he can't go to the Ranch. If you've got five years and you're a Level 1 you wouldn't be sent to the Ranch because of the potentiality of escape is very high. Any sexual offenses can preclude an inmate from going to the Ranch. No rapists, molesters, or inmates convicted of serious sexual crimes. There are two kinds of crimes — property crimes or personal crimes — which determine an inmate's level.

Control Points and Facilities

4 Post

This is an old round brick building in the middle of the prison courtyard. It's the first or last exit point where there's contact with prison staff. 4 Post is set up to control prison foot traffic. If inmates gets too close, they're asked immediately what their business is that brings them there, because the main gate "door" is just 100 feet away and that's freedom to an inmate.

Max (maximum security) Shack

The Max Shack is a crowd control or a point where the officers separate the inmates from the upper to lower yards. Some inmates are allowed to go to the lower yard during certain hours. It's also a point of separation for the industry workers. Some of the industry workers who live and sleep in the main facility get to the Max Shack, get identified as a prison worker, and then proceed down to the lower yard to go to the prison industries so that they can go to their jobs.

It was also historically the end of San Quentin. The prison stopped at that point back in the dark days. The Q was built over time in several steps. That was the farthest southern point of the old prison.

At the far end of the yard is the yard office, another location where officers, lieutenants, and sergeants could, can, and would stop in and have a place of their own.

Education Room

The Education Room in the North Block is across from the Max Shack in the upper yard where lectures, talks, music, and art classes take place. Some teachers give the inmates pre-release classes. Inmates who are getting really close to getting released back to the community will be given talks to remind them how complex it is in the free world as opposed of how simple it is in prison where an inmate is told what time to eat, when to eat, where to eat, and what he's going to eat. He doesn't have to make change, or deal with people other than those in his own environment, which is all its own subculture. He lives the cartoon life that inmates live when they tell each other their stories. It almost always turns out that, although the guy tells the other inmates (his peers) that it was $5,000 that he got from the store robbery, it was only $7.80. They're also reminded during pre-release talks how to get jobs, how to dress, how to talk to people in this (free) world. If they get upset with something or someone, they're taught how to deal with anger (so don't stab a waitress over a bad meal).

Terminology

Bed Count

By California state law inmates have to be counted four times a day and some inmates are counted more. Sex offenders are counted even more often. All beds are assigned to specific individuals so consequently they are counted several times a day and in various locations. The bed count is how many beds does the prison have. The question then becomes how many inmates does the prison have? There could be a cell that has two bunks in it but it's got broken plumbing so the cell can't be used. The bed count remains constant but the number of inmates in that unit can vary because of how many beds are available and what kind of inmates they are. The prison can't house just anybody with anybody. The prison has to house serious offenders away from guys that are less serious offenders. So the bed count in each unit may have more or fewer inmates depending on the various elements. The bed count is a very big deal.

IMS (Inmate Movement Sheet)

On a daily basis, by law, the State of California has to show where inmates are at all times. Information on activities or programs, such as music, art, or working in the factories, is published daily on the daily inmate movement sheet (IMS). It will have the inmates' name, number, assignment, the hour or time, and where they're expected to be at that hour. So at 4 Post and the Max Shack, the officers can check the inmate movement sheet (IMS) against where the inmate is going.

How About a Gig at San Quentin State Prison?

September 8, 1998

Driving to San Quentin Prison for the first time is a crazy ride for me. All I can think of are the four rules everyone has to remember before entering the prison: Rule number one: People from the outside cannot wear denim. No blue jeans. It is the cloth of the inmates. The colors to wear are black, green, white, gray or brown. Blue and red are not allowed in prison because they are gang colors. Rule number two: Do not ever run or even walk too fast while working inside the prison grounds. Otherwise the guards will think that something is wrong and start shooting. The prison motto is "Shoot first; ask questions later." That is the golden rule for the guards at Quentin. Rule number three: Always have a picture ID on yourself at all times. If you cannot prove who you really are, the guards will not let you leave the prison. Rule number four is: No hostage is recognized so if there is a riot in the prison, no staff is going to help you. Kiss your ass goodbye, my friend. I have been told that during a prison riot I'm on my own. No deals are going to be made on my behalf. Those are the four golden rules to live by while working or teaching inside of the prison. I had to sign a piece of paper saying that I understood the four rules. For a guy who has never even been in the back of a police car or been in jail I must say that this job was a pretty ballsy one for me to take on.

When I pull my truck up to the east gate entrance it takes my breath away. I begin having hot and cold flashes every couple of seconds. After signing my name in the prison logbook,

I'm searched by the officer on duty and then cleared to enter the prison grounds. I try my hardest not to freak out as I walk through the prison courtyard. The sight of hundreds of inmates dressed in blue denim is staggering. The whole prison looks like a big sea of blue denim. Most of the inmates have lots of tattoos. As I begin walking past some of the officers on duty or the inmates walking around, I keep thinking of the questions that I have about prison life. I have only been in San Quentin Prison less than ten minutes and I'm already getting this creepy feeling running down the back of my neck to my toes. As it is my first night on the job I am still a little unsure of some things, like what not to say to the officers or inmates. I try not to look too stupid in front of the staff. I am very green about prison life but that is all going to change real quickly. This place is crazy. A kind of circus from hell.

By mistake I call an officer in Quentin a guard. This officer turns around with his eyes popping out of his head and shouts back to me at the top of his lungs "Guards work at department stores like Kmart or Wal-Mart. Now, officers work in the prisons. It's better than being in the military. It's a great job! Son, don't you ever forget: guards Wal-Mart, officers prisons! Got it?"

All I can think to myself is the state couldn't pay me enough money to work as an officer in this prison. I have also been reading the prison staff handbook issued to all the workers and volunteers. It says never get too friendly with any inmates. Never tell them anything about where you live, your family, or anything about yourself.

As my boss greets me, she explains to me that she will be with me in the Education Room while I'm teaching music to the inmates; she figures seven to ten times on Tuesday nights. She goes on to say she'll be going through paperwork in the next room with the door open. She says with a little grin on her face, "I'm here to make sure that you're safe, not scared, and if you have any questions about the program or the Q, I'll be right here to help you through it." As we are walking to the Education Room she gives me the inmate movement sheet and explains about some of my new inmate music students I'm about to meet. She tells me that the inmates who are housed at North Block, or as most staff call it, "The Hill," are mostly lifers.

Some of the inmates who signed up for this music class own their guitars, while other inmates have to sign a prison form in order to get a state prison-owned guitar. All prison-owned guitars and other instruments in North Block are stored in the Education Room unless the inmate has followed procedures to bring his guitar back into his cell or housing unit. It's also my understanding that most of the inmates in my music class have been locked up in San Quentin Prison for over ten years.

The room used for music and art classes is in the oldest part of the prison. Seeing it is like going back in time because San Quentin Prison is the oldest prison in California. The Education Room smells old and musty. The windows are always shut and locked. Once I open up the door to air out the room, the inmates start showing up. The first five minutes of the first music class are a really big wake-up call for me. There is a kind of smell in prison that the inmates give off. It's a strong scent of cheap food and sweat. I could cut it with a knife, it's so bad. My heart is pumping pretty fast. It takes everything I can do not to cry or throw up as I watch inmates and officers walking around the room just looking at each other. Every inmate has at least ten tattoos each, some on their head, neck, face or knuckles. Some of the inmates almost look blue.

I have eight students in class. Some of the inmates already play the guitar pretty well, while others don't have a clue. I break into a huge smile watching the inmates introduce themselves to each other. After meeting my students, the first song I have them play is "Old Time Rock-n-Roll." The inmates seem to enjoy banging on their guitars while trying to sing and dance at the same time.

So for the next two-and-a-half hours, we all rock out together. From time to time, an inmate looks up from his guitar and says, "Wow, I almost forgot that I'm locked up in a prison." As the night goes on, I begin to look at the faces of the inmates in the classroom.

While some look like the boy next door, a lot of them look like they would kill you right there. I would not want to piss off any of them.

The air does not move in the room much. Since the door is always shut and locked, the Education Room has the fragrance of a boys' locker room. The smell of underarm is sometimes unbearable for me. It makes my eyes water and my nose plug up. But most of the inmates are really hungry to learn anything about the guitar. They really seem to care about the music class.

After the class ends, all the inmates either shake my hand or gave me a big high five before walking out of the room. The one thing that I noticed in class tonight was the little boy look of being lost on all of their faces. Music seems to be the common ground for all the inmates in class. To see these inmates working with each other through music is just a miracle.

As I walk back to my truck, my mind races a thousand miles an hour. What a wild ride prison is. Three hours of non-stop rushes, guns, tattoos, and music. My first night of music with the inmates at San Quentin Prison. The land of forgotten souls. My body is numb the whole ride home. My head is killing me. The pain is so bad I want to throw up, but I can't wait to see the looks on the kids' faces in Juvenile Hall tomorrow when I tell them about teaching music to the inmates in San Quentin Prison. The kids in Juvenile Hall all want to come to prison. It's insane but some boys think that prison is a cool place. I'm going to tell them that they need to know what it's really like.

Some boys have grown up thinking that prison life is a very macho lifestyle. Three meals a day for free, you can hang out with your home boyz and family members while working out. If you are a gang member you assume everything will be great, kick back and have some fun. Street kids think it's all about now. What is in it for them? Most are starved for attention. It's a twisted way of thinking but to these kids it is real. It's their way of thinking.

None of the boys in Juvenile Hall would stand a chance in prison. The older inmates thrive on the younger inmates. It's a power thing. A new inmate can be bought for a pack of gum or about anything you can think of. Everything in prison has its price, it all depends on how much you are willing to pay. It's a kid's worst nightmare.

In the real world no man is going to tell his brother, friend, relative or fellow gang members outside of the walls that he was raped in prison. That shows weakness and that's the last thing any inmate wants other people to know. One has to have a damaged soul in order to desire the prison lifestyle.

September 22, 1998

This is my second time coming to San Quentin Prison to teach. Driving the forty-five minutes gives me a lot of time to think about things like the day-to-day stuff that goes on behind the walls, or what it's really like living life in a cage. I must say I have played music all my life in all kinds of places in every kind of event you could think of. But this place takes the prize. This is the strangest gig yet. The more I think about the Q, the more cold rushes I get running through my body.

As I enter from the east gate of San Quentin, the view of the Bay Bridge, Oakland and the sunset on the bay water is stunning. Lots of color in contrast to the baby-shit yellow the prison is painted. The houses in San Quentin village are prime real estate, probably the best in the North Bay with a billion-dollar view. But how someone could live next to a state prison is beyond me. I could not do it.

After tonight's roll call we go through "Old Time Rock-n-Roll" from last week, and then I show the group "Hit the Road Jack" and "Stand By Me." Again the music class goes very smoothly; everyone has a great time and a couple of the inmates ask me if they can sing more songs like "Jail House Rock" and "Folsom Prison Blues." I laugh to myself, thinking about their choice of tunes.

As I'm walking out tonight I see two inmates with yellow jump suits on being brought in. They have two officers on each side. Both look very young, mean, and scared for their lives. I can't imagine the first night being locked up in a cage. I have already heard a couple of stories floating around here about young boys coming into the prison for the first time and crying all night long. They were marked for the rest of their stay in the Q, labeled as weak pussies from that point on. Crying in prison is not a smart thing for inmates. Be strong, otherwise you'll become dead meat, always looking over your shoulder. Not being safe in this kind of place is a nightmare. Trust no one is the main rule and do not get too friendly. Never let your guard down. This is a city where time stands still, while life goes on without you just beyond the walls of the Q.

September 29, 1998

It's my third time coming to San Quentin. I thought I would stop having that sick feeling rush through my body every time I drive to the Q, but I'm wrong. It is getting creepier with every visit. As always, I drive to the staff parking lot. Each time I walk up the twenty-five stairs, go past three check points, get cleared, and only then can I enter the main post of San Quentin Prison. I sign in, the officer checks me and my guitar case for guns or drugs. After all that, I'm given the okay to wait till they're ready for me. "Hurry and wait." After five more minutes, the officer smiles at me and says welcome to San Quentin State Prison. Enjoy your stay and be safe. Next! I'm put in yet another holding cage, which smells really old. Everything in the Q is old, even the sign-in log book. There is an officer that sits in an office and controls all opening and closing of doors, gates and the prison driveway front entrance. They buzz you in; they buzz you out. Does not matter who you are or where you work. It's a house rule for every one who enters or exits the prison. That is only one of a number of rules here in San Quentin.

The last door to open before entering the main courtyard at the Q is the biggest steel door that I have ever seen outside of Disneyland. As I open that huge door it becomes another land, another lifestyle, the land of incarceration. Each time I feel like Dorothy from "The Wizard of Oz." I get that feeling of mellow madness here at the Q. Very unsettling. A quiet storm ready to explode at any given moment. Tonight's roll call is easy. Ten students in class tonight. The songs are "Mustang Sally," "Workin' Man Blues" and "Hit the Road Jack." There is nothing like hearing ten inmates singing "Ride Sally Ride" in bad three-part harmony.

The class is coming together a lot faster than I thought it would. So far, nothing has gone wrong for me. No fights in class and I've never had to call for any kind of help, thank God.

I'm told by one of my students that new inmates coming into San Quentin are given yellow jumpsuits to wear. They have to be processed; given all their paperwork, prison clothes, shoes, prison number and their cell unit. I'm told new inmates are arriving night and day at all hours. The Q is now being used as a kind of holding tank for other prisons throughout the State of California.

I am sure glad I can leave this place at night and go home to be with my family. I hope I'm never caught in the middle of a riot, or worse yet, a lock down. No one likes being locked up. The feeling I get while being here at the Q is of a human zoo. I wonder how many inmates have gone crazy while being caged up in their cells. Living inside the prison, always having someone from staff or other inmates telling you what to do. This is now the family. This is now your home for a long, long time. What a lost feeling knowing that life will never be the same again. Being treated worse than a dog. Having officers barking if you walk past the yellow tape on the prison floor.

At about ten minutes to nine, I tell the group to put away their chairs, get their guitars and music, and with ten high fives my third music class at San Quentin Prison is over. As I walk back across the prison courtyard, I can hear the sounds of the foghorn coming from the Bay. Looking up at the sky, I see the moon is full and bright. The stars are twinkling. I can see and hear freedom. Once I arrive at that big steel door I open it up and walk inside for the first of many checkpoints I have to go back through in order to leave. The door slams loudly behind me like a big bang on the Fourth of July. I am buzzed back out, patted down, and my guitar case is checked. Then I have to sign out of the logbook before being allowed to leave. After everything is done — all the paper work and check outs — I'm told by the officer on duty at the east gate to have a wonderful night driving home, to be safe and that he will see me next Tuesday.

Driving home I keep thinking, now I know how a lion or a monkey feels living in a zoo. It's got to be a bad nightmare living in prison. Some men will die here. Outside, a lot of boys cannot wait to get their turn to live here. I hope by coming to San Quentin and teaching music to the inmates, I can bring lots of reality stories back to the tough boys at risk that I work with. I could never understand why someone would want to live in prison. Life is odd in that way. Some kids have strange goals for their future.

October 20, 1998

It's my fourth time here at San Quentin Prison. I have had the last three weeks to think about what it means to be doing a prison music class. When some of my friends and family members found out about me working at the Q, I was asked what is it like behind the walls? What do the inmates look like? Has anyone hit on you yet? So far I have been asked almost everything about the Q. I just tell them it's a crazy little city to visit.

So many stories have been written and movies made about the Q, that it's wild for me to be working in this place teaching a music program. Life in prison is like living in a sea of lost souls. Everyone is swimming in an ocean of loneliness where the code of brotherhood among raccs runs very high. An eye for an eye is the main rule of living life behind the walls of San Quentin State Prison. It's a dog-eat-dog world. Anyone can be turned into an animal when he is locked up in a cage for hours.

I've been telling the kids in Juvenile Hall about prison life, hoping that some kids are getting the real picture. It's not a nice place to live. I've only been here a few times and already I'm feeling the strain. Some of the tough boys at the hall still think prison life is a joke. Somehow it will be cool for them. They would not get beat up or gang raped. Hopefully the kids that I'm working with will never end up here. Some seem to be listening to my words a little closer now, which is a great start. I pray those kids will never have to find out for themselves. I hope to get over this feeling that has been burning in my stomach every time I enter San Quentin Prison. Will it ever go away?

Tonight my students inform me that North Block in the Q is having a talent show. Kind of like a bad prison Gong Show. The inmates say they will be performing some of the songs I have been teaching them. One inmate tells me they are calling themselves "Buzzy's Boyz." I'm feeling like some of these inmates are slowly starting to trust me a little more. I can see in a matter of time this class will be up and running with lots of rock-n-roll songs.

It's hot tonight walking into the prison but even hotter once I get inside the Education Room. I have no fresh air to breathe and the sweat rolls down my face. Sitting in the chair with no fans, wow, I feel like it's one of those hot summer, muggy Midwestern nights. I don't mind being hot. I'm very used to heat. But this kind of heat is nuts. I wonder how hot the inmates' cells can get.

Before class starts, an older black inmate comes in to clean the room and take out the trash, simple house cleaning. He tells me that today is his birthday. He is now seventy-two. A lifer. Never leaving this place. He asks me, "Could you sing 'Happy Birthday' to me, son? Would you do that for an old black con?" So with that I pull out my guitar and play the song. While I'm singing "Happy Birthday" to him, his eyes water up and, yes, so do mine. It moves me that he cried because of me singing a simple song just for him. I am truly blessed to be given this gift to teach music, much less in a prison. Singing to that old black con was my gift to him. Birthdays in prison must be very sad for the inmates' families. Just another day inside the walls of the Q.

Tonight is my first time ever hearing whistles and alarms going off in prison. There is nothing like hearing the sound of keys swinging back and forth with officers running past the Education

Room, while all the inmates began to sit down on the floor. The alarms sound a lot like those air raid sirens of WWII. No one talks; if you did, no one would hear you. My face must have turned white. I have that blank look on it because one of the inmates stands up, waves his hand at me and says with a grin on his face, "Hey Buzzy, don't worry about this shit going on outside. If you don't hear the sounds of guns being shot off, then it's okay. If you just stay put in the prison Education Room you'll be fine." The only words I can muster out of my mouth are "wonderful, just what my wife is going to love to hear."

I'm finding out pretty damn fast that this Education Room in prison is a safe place for these inmates. But it's also a very safe place for me too. I'm pleased by that little bit of information. After everything calms down outside, I begin to take roll call. One of the female officers comes into the Education Room and starts barking out her own roll call. I forgot my pen so I ask her if I can borrow a pen from her. No reply. I'm thinking maybe she didn't hear me or I'm not sure if she's blowing me off, about my request. I notice one of my students giving me the look like "stop right now, don't ask or say another word, just drop it. She's not going to help you look." So I do; I just stop. So when she leaves the room that same student stands up and hands me his pen to use. I now have entered these inmates' circle of trust. I'm not sure if that's a good or a bad thing. Never bond or side with inmates or officers. Just ride the fence right down the middle of the road.

I stop by the prison's church office and introduce myself to the chaplain on duty. He tells me that all of the inmates in my music class love and respect the fact that I'm even coming into the prison to teach music. The chaplain tells me the inmates call me "a free man," kind of a medicine man of music. He says that when I bring in the music it heals the souls of the inmates in the Q.

He goes on to say that one of my students has been locked up in San Quentin Prison for the past seventeen years. Now that's a long time to be living in a cage. Before walking away I say, "Thank you for your kind words, chaplain. I hope that we can talk again some time. Have a good night." The chaplain smiles and then whispers these words to me, really slow, "If you hear guns being shot off just lie down on the ground. Close your eyes and pray. Now go my child of the music. Go now and teach those inmates the power of music, my son. May God bless you and keep you safe while working here."

As I walk away, I keep thinking what could happen next? This place is like the circus from hell. The songs for the inmates tonight are "Mustang Sally" and "I Feel Good." It's pretty cool to have my prison students talking, laughing and feeling good about this music class and themselves. This room is a safe place to let their guard down and have some good clean fun.

Some of the officers on duty tell me that a lot of young black kids from around the Oakland area are now showing up in the Q. They also say that they have seen their share of young boys coming in from all over the state. In some cases it's better to have them here in San Quentin than where they are staying now. Some of the new tough kid gang bangers think prison is going to be a joy ride. Sitting around kicking it with their homies. Not a care in the world. Three meals a day, no big deal. Then they enter the real world of prison life. Once you enter San Quentin Prison as an inmate everything changes. There is no going back. You can't turn back the clock and start over; nor can you go home to cry to mommy or daddy. Welcome to Camp Quentin kiddies! You now have a new best friend and cell mate. Hope you two can get along with each other. So remember kids, you did the crime; now grow up; become a man; greet your new life behind the walls of the Q.

I have been told by both the staff and some of the officers that a lot of these inmates will most likely return to prison within a year or even sooner. Once you are labeled a felon or ex-felon, your life will change. It's harder to find work and housing. Living in the free world without being told what to do is also hard for some of the inmates. I wonder if it's because a lot of kids have grown up without their dads being around talking to them or loving them. Just giving them a little TLC. So those kids act out and grow up to become pissed-off inmates with no hope of feeling what it is like to live your dreams. (If they ever had any in the first place.)

After class is over and everyone is putting away their guitars, I walk over to the drinking fountain and push the button. Just as the water is about to enter my mouth, one of the inmates in class says with a big grin, "Boss I wouldn't be drinking the water here at the Q. I've heard that there's a lot of lead in the water system. Worse yet, we've been hearing stories for years that the officers put saltpeter in the water. Nobody ever drinks the water straight out of the fountain." With that my thumb shoots back away from that fountain. But now I have a mouth full of toxic water. Without missing a beat, I spit the water out of my mouth splashing it everywhere. As I turn to say thank you for saving me from getting sick, everyone in the room is laughing so hard a couple of inmates almost piss their pants. Then that same inmate says to me, "I got you Buzzy. Pretty funny. I had you going for a few minutes, didn't I?" Once again the inmates have had a great big laugh on ole Uncle Buzzy.

On my way out, I pass some offices that catch my eye. Three office doors have odd signs hanging on each of their doorknobs. Their words are very moving, but profoundly sad. The first one reads "Work Incentive Program." Door two reads "Friends outside of the walls." Door three reads "Men's Advisory Council." I have a hard time even sitting in one place for too long so I could not imagine how crazy the mind must get after years and years of being locked up. It has got to weigh hard on these inmates' souls, knowing they are never going to leave this place.

As I reach the last check point before leaving tonight, I'm reminded of how much I love this job working with a class of people that the rest of mankind seems to have given up on. To give them some self worth through music and show them how to feel good about themselves. It's not a lot, but it is something. It's giving back a little something to the world.

October 27, 1998

It's my wife's birthday and it is also my fifth guitar class at San Quentin. Happy Birthday, honey, I sure hope I'm never working in prison on my birthday. It would not be very cool hearing the inmates singing to me; that's not my kind of birthday party. "Happy B Day Dear Buzzy," are not the words I really want to hear in prison.

Halloween is just around the corner so tonight the song is "The Monster Mash." A cool little tune with a kick. As I walk into the courtyard, a light rain is falling, the air is cold and the fog is rolling in pretty thick. The prison takes on a very spooky look at night. It kind of reminds me of the old black and white monster movies of the 1950s. As I walk I can hear the foghorn blowing through the wind. In the few times that I have come to the prison, I have learned a couple of things that help get me through while working behind the walls. It's simple. Try and get along with everyone — officers, inmates, staff — anyone who is behind the walls with you, try and get along with them. Give the officers and inmates respect and they will mostly give it back in return.

Tonight, class is small, only five inmates, all white. The black inmates are on lock down, so teaching five students how to play and sing "The Monster Mash" is pretty easy for the most part. Two of the students try to sing like Bela Lugosi and Wolfman Jack. What a sight! Just like little boys having clean fun, laughing, carrying on like children with a new toy. When it's time to stop and put away our guitars, one of my students tells me that he is going to be released in a little over two weeks. He also says he does not ever want to return to the prison, plus he hopes that he will be able to keep his shit together this time out or otherwise he will be looking at life next time. He has two kids, both boys. I ask him "How long have you been in San Quentin?" His reply is "Four years longer than I should have done; eight years four months and ten days is a long time for robbing and stabbing someone, if you ask me, a little stiff. Don't you think the judge could have cut me a little slack? The other guy was an asshole. He owed me money for some drugs that I had bought from him and he didn't come through. So one thing leads to another. The next thing I know I'm being dragged off by three cops in handcuffs. I knew I was fucked, so here I am, end of story. I'll never do drugs again. That's what got me here in the first place. So wish me luck Buzzy cause I'm going to need all the luck I can get."

We all shake hands, say our good-byes till next week, and I make my trip back to the main entrance of the prison. After dark, the Q takes on the look of Count Dracula's castle. Creepy, very evil, a cold feeling like bad juju. But all it takes is one of these inmates telling me how much this music class has helped change his life around in good ways; that is inspiring to me. It does move me to tears sometimes.

Driving home tonight all I can think about is the word freedom and how we take it for granted. Do the things that you want to do in your lifetime because it only comes around once, baby. That is all one gets. I have realized this while working with the inmates in San Quentin, plus the kids in the hall and the ones who live on the streets. I hope those boys never have the fate of seeing the inside of the prison walls. It would break their souls.

How can we as caring people be more loving and get more involved with the boys and girls at risk in California to help them stop and to break this cycle that is killing young kids on the streets and sending children to prisons? Bringing music to the inmates at San Quentin and the boys and girls in Juvenile Hall is just my way of helping out. Well, I will try again next week with yet another song for my students in prison music class at San Quentin.

November 3, 1998

It's election day. So the big question now is who is going to be the next Governor of the State of California and do these inmates at San Quentin really give a shit what goes on outside of the walls, let alone who's running our state? As I walk through the prison courtyard going to class tonight I can hear the officers on duty barking out orders to the inmates. Things like when to eat, what time a class is going to start, and what time to go to bed. I get a feeling of being locked away in a concentration boot camp for misfits. As I walk past the Max Shack, after getting my paper work for roll call and signing in, I find myself less nervous than the last few times I was here. I'm hoping it's going to get easier as time goes on.

In the time that I've been doing this class, there have been three lock downs, mostly due to gang fighting. Last week's lock down came from an inmate stabbing another inmate with a homemade knife, called a shank. Plus, one of the officers on duty had gotten beaten up pretty badly by an inmate. But that's what happens when people are put in cages to live their life like a bunch of monkeys; this bunch is wild and mean like street animals. Gutter rats, that's what people outside the walls of prison call mankind's inmates of justice. I have to wonder to myself what crimes brought my music students into prison? Drugs? Murder? Rape? These inmates have very little or no self worth. How sad. I've been trying to keep this class fun and still give these inmates some kind of hard homework to study to keep them focused on something positive when I'm not able to come to the prison.

The songs tonight are "Who'll Stop the Rain" and "Santa Claus Is Coming to Town." I only have four students. Very, very mellow. I'm kind of glad to have it that way once in a while. Around 8:00 p.m. the door opens up and this big black inmate pops his bald head inside the room to see what is happening. As he looks around the room, he never smiles once, but right before he says goodbye, he looks me straight in the eyes and barks out "You, Guitar Man, keep bringing in the music. It mellows these assholes out. Later, girls." With that the door closes, leaving us to start work.

As the class is singing "Santa Claus Is Coming to Town," I see something that will be burned in my mind forever. As I look up towards the prison catwalk, two officers pop their heads in front of this huge plate glass window to watch us. What a picture! A full moon, fog rolling by very slowly, and then for a few minutes a light rain falls on the prison windows making dirty streaks run down the glass. I'm holding a guitar; the officers are holding guns. I don't think I could ever get used to having officers always looking over my shoulders. Not my kind of lifestyle. After class has ended, one of my students asks me if I write my own songs and if so, could I sing one for them. So I sing and play three of my own songs, one of which is called "Please Come Home," written for Polly Klaas, the little girl who was kidnapped and murdered in Northern California.

The look on their faces is really something. When I sing the Polly song for them, there is not a dry eye in the classroom. Two of my older students have to blow their noses and wipe their eyes, while the other two inmates hold their faces in their hands. They must all have kids to react that way. The guy that killed Polly Klaas is now on Death Row in San Quentin Prison. His name is Richard Allen Davis and he is hated by a lot of inmates in prisons all around California because he is the person responsible for the new three strikes law for repeat offenders as well as for killing a child. The prisons are now overflowing because of this law. When class is over, I walk past some of my students who are either standing or sitting, just waiting to be given the word to return to their cells. Most inmates are smoking cheap, hand-rolled cigarettes while talking about tonight's music class. Others just sit on the ground strumming their guitars.

As I enter the last checkpoint before leaving the prison, it seems almost too mellow, with sea gulls flying around and a cool breeze blowing through my hair. I'm glad I can walk out of this place and drive home. I've got to say that it was very cool to see my students smiling, laughing, and singing songs, acting like little boys in class tonight. Maybe in some cases they never laughed at all as children. I don't think the inmates get a chance to feel this way very often. In the night shadows, as the moon glows, the officers watch everyone from the catwalk while they cast down that heavy vibe of "Don't even try anything stupid or else" look. What a strange land to visit. I am the Doctor of Music in the land of incarceration. What will next week's class be like?

December 1, 1998

This is my seventh time coming into the Q teaching music. I've had to miss the last three weeks of class because I have not been given my green prison ID card, yet. I'm hoping it arrives soon. My boss has been my escort for the last seven times, but then she called in sick. I can't be left alone with the inmates yet. I need to build up their trust and also make sure I feel okay being all by myself in a room full of inmates locked away in a prison. The other reason I couldn't come in was because there was an execution just last week. All inmates are put on hard-core lockdown. It must be a strange vibe in San Quentin walking around as an officer on a lockdown shift, all the inmates locked away in their cells. Heavy!

It's creepy walking through the east gate entrance tonight because just last Tuesday, I was watching TV and people were carrying signs, crying and praying, protesting the execution. Some feel that is the law and it does not matter much that inmates are put to death.

After signing in tonight and getting my roll call sheet taken care of, I make my way to the Education Room for class. Five inmates are waiting outside for me with guitars in hand and a look on their faces like sad little boys. My boss opens up the door of the room, letting out that smell of dead air. The kind of air that smells like a boy's arm pit after he has been running for an hour. After about ten minutes of tuning the guitars, I show the inmates how to play "Jingle Bells" and "Blue Christmas." Within an hour of working out the words to "Blue Christmas," all five inmates take turns singing in their best Elvis voice for everyone else in the class. What a sight to see! Inmates dancing, walking and moving their hips like Elvis. Thank you very much! The song "Jingle Bells" makes everyone smile, I think because it reminds most of them of their childhood. Christmas songs have a way of bringing you back to being a little kid again when the only worry you had was pissing off your mom if she caught you looking under the Christmas tree or coming home late for dinner.

When 9:00 p.m. rolls around, the door to the Education Room opens up; two big officers walk in and say "Okay ladies, it's time to wrap it up and go to bed. Bed count is in twenty minutes." So each inmate takes his guitar and files out of the room, one by one. As I'm closing the door behind me, one of the officers on duty says, "Hey Guitar Man, thanks for coming in and bringing music to this place. I know these inmates really look forward to this class, and that alone can keep a man from going crazy."

As we both say our good-byes and shake hands I realize that a lot of the inmates I'm working with are lifers who are never going to leave this prison alive. Driving home, all I can think of is those five inmates singing "Blue Christmas" like Elvis. My wife will never believe tonight's stories. Jailhouse rock-n-roll with a twist of Elvis.

December 15, 1998

It's a big night for me. This will be the first time I have ever been alone with the inmates. Just the inmates and myself. No boss, no officers. Just this little whistle and my guitar. Wish me good luck. Another cold and foggy night in San Quentin as I walk in, sign my name, and pass all the checkpoints, to be let inside the prison. It always takes me at least ten to twenty minutes to get signed in and cleared, sometimes longer. As I get closer to the Education Room door, by the Max Shack, an old black inmate with two gold teeth smiles at me and says, "Merry Christmas, boss, you got a smoke?" All I can say is, "I'm sorry, sir, I don't smoke." His eyes light up like two full moons and with a grin, he says to me, "Son, did you just call me sir? Because in the Q, no con or inmate is ever called sir, Thank you and may God bless you." As that old man walks away, I can't help wonder how long he's been here.

One by one the students come into the room, just like little boys with their sixth grade teacher; they all thank me and give me a Christmas card they have made for me. It feels very mellow tonight in the Q. A peaceful calmness. Christmas is in the air. The songs tonight are "Rockin' Around the Christmas Tree" and "Deck the Halls," both words and music. I must say all eight inmates never sounded better as a group; everyone sings and plays his heart out. It tests my soul coming to the Q and teaching music, guitar and singing to inmates who have very little or nothing in their lives to look forward to. I'm glad to give back the gift of music to anyone that needs happiness in his life. At ten minutes to nine, the whole class sings "White Christmas," not once, but three times at the top of their lungs. Christmas in San Quentin. When the class comes to a close everyone again wishes me and my family a happy Christmas while shaking my hand goodbye. In my heart I feel so sad for these inmates' families, knowing that on Christmas Eve the children of inmates in prisons all over California will be going to bed without their dads to hug them and tell them Merry Christmas. That's got to be tough on the kids and even tougher on the moms.

Walking back out of San Quentin Prison I hear a choir singing Christmas songs in the prison church. Some of the songs are "White Christmas," "Silent Night," and "Little Town of Bethlehem." I find myself singing along. There I am, like Gene Kelly in "Singing in the Rain," snapping my fingers and tapping my feet all the time a fine mist of rain is falling on the church window. I want to open the church door and join in. I can feel my spirits lifting even higher, when a passing officer walks up to me and says, "What the hell are you doing? You're the first person I've ever seen dancing in prison and it's raining. Are you fucking nuts or what?" I say, "Hey, I'm sorry for dancing. I will never do it again, I promise." With that, the officer barks, "Move along, son, and Merry Christmas. Now go home."

Before I can be let back out of the prison, I have to go through this huge cell, a big holding tank for people coming and going from outside. There have been a few moments when I have felt this cold rush all over my body. It always seems to happen when I hear the sound of a big bang as the cell door slams shut. I start saying my good-byes when I notice the prison TV monitor hanging on the wall right above the main entrance of the Q. It reads "Merry Christmas and Welcome to San Quentin State Prison" in big bright letters. What a joke! At the last checkpoint, I see ten inmates, all chained together, all wearing white jumpsuits, being loaded into the prison van. I ask the officer on duty, "What is that all about" and he says, "These are the knuckleheads that have done their time for their fuck-ups. But you can bet your life on this, out of those ten, eight will be back in here within a year or sooner."

By the time that I reach my truck, my emotions are running pretty high. This place could make any man crazy. How many inmates do you think have become insane while doing their time in San Quentin? A better question to ask is out of one hundred percent of the inmates who enter the Q, how many return? I thank God every Tuesday night while driving home from prison for giving me and my family love, happiness and the joy of freedom.

January 5, 1999

The sky is grey and it's raining pretty hard. It's normal winter weather here in Northern California. On the drive to San Quentin tonight traffic is light and it only takes me ten minutes to get inside the Q. I have to wait for my paper work to clear, but that only takes about two minutes. After getting the okay to enter and sign in, I make my way to the Education Room. While dodging raindrops, I can see my breath, it's that cold. There are a few inmates walking around the prison courtyard, talking to each other or waiting to be let into the prison dining hall. Waiting for anything in prison is the challenge. Everyone lives by the hour.

I have four more times left on my contract to teach music here at the Q. I must say that I am very blown away by the vibe in prison. Every hour in here is a lifetime of pain. This place is the House of Doom. As I set up the room for class, three inmates show up with their guitars dripping wet but ready to learn a song or two. After roll call is done, I only have those three inmates. No one else shows up, so I take my time to show my students the songs "King of the Road," "Twist and Shout" and "Born to Be Wild." It works out to be one song for each sudent. The class is the mellowest that I have ever had. No big deal. Just before 8:45, I have each student play and sing his song for the class. The first inmate sings "King of the Road" and doesn't sing too badly. The next student does "Born to Be Wild." And then all of us sing the song "Twist and Shout" so the last inmate can play the guitar. They laugh and enjoy themselves all night. One of the inmates says to me, "I wish that you could stay a little longer. When you're here, we forget that we're in prison. You bring peace and comfort into this hell hole and we respect you for that." As the clock hits 9:00 p.m. sharp, two officers open up the door and say, "It's time to move. Bed count is in five minutes." All those inmates move fast, first putting away their music and then their guitars. They have to walk down the stairs and out the door, then walk across the main yard and end up at their cell just in time for bed count.

Night after night it's the same boring thing; nothing changes. Life here is always going to be looking over your shoulder and being told what to do. As I drive home, I pray the kids I'll be seeing tomorrow in Juvenile Hall will never end up here with their souls broken, wondering how to live like wild dogs or gutter rats marking out and guarding their territory.

As the lights of San Quentin fade away in the mist of the night rain, I'm reminded of how lucky my life has turned out. I'm blessed to be playing and teaching music and getting paid for it.

January 12, 1999

This is my ninth time coming into San Quentin Prison and teaching the music class. I feel honored and very humbled to have this chance to go behind the walls of the Q and teach music to the inmates. I'm blown away by how much I have learned about prison life in just nine weeks of classes. Twenty-eight hours of teaching inmates how to play guitar and sing songs. It has been a phenomenal experience for me, but what is crazy are the stories that I'm bringing back to the kids locked up at the Hall. Sometimes the only difference between prison and Juvenile Hall is the fact that officers in San Quentin carry guns and time in prison stands still. Nothing moves fast in the Q, nothing except for officers in the middle of a lock down. The more I come into the Q the more buildings I am noticing.

The buildings are old and real cold looking. The vibe I get, in Quentin is one of coldness, loneliness with nothing to do but wait for tomorrow to come.

As I check in tonight my boss tells me, "Buzzy, you're doing so well, I've got some great news for you. You've been given twelve more weeks for your next music class at a place here in San Quentin. It's called H-Unit." With two classes left on my contract, I am overjoyed; coming to prison once a week is such a rush for me. Tonight it is cold, foggy and raining. When it's gray skies in prison, the vibe is much sadder. After roll call is over, I have eight students in class ready to play music. The songs tonight are "Runaway" and "I Fought the Law," by request. One of my students tells me, "Hey Buzzy, I've been playing my guitar sometimes ten hours a day, seven days a week."

As we go through the song "Runaway" I have one inmate sing the words while the other inmates play their guitars. He sounds like a bad Tom Jones, but he smiles the whole time he sings and everyone in the room laughs as he dances around the chairs.

Right before class ends, one of the students puts his hand in the air and yells, "Time out, girls, I've got something to tell Buzzy. We all want to thank you for coming in here and teaching guitar. It makes all of us inmates here in class feel like we're something other than a fucking number." That inmate also says the other inmates in class are starting to have a little more self-esteem for the first time in their lives, all through playing the guitar. He goes on to say that he loves coming to music class because it really helps him escape from the pressures of being locked up in prison every day; with only eighteen months left to serve, the music class sounds like a really great time-killer to him. I can see how easily feelings in prison can be turned into friendships, but that is a bad thing while working with inmates. Never bring the job home. The San Quentin Handbook warns against any kind of buddy buddy stuff going on between teachers, officers, or inmates; otherwise bad things could happen and the last thing I need is for some inmate to look me up when he gets out. The red lights would be flashing everywhere; my wife would not be happy at all.

As I'm driving out of the prison staff parking lot, I can hear bells going off and officers screaming, "There's a fight going on!" Another wild night of chaos in the land of San Quentin Prison. I shake my head wondering if I am really making a difference with my music class at the Q or with the kids I work with in Juvenile Hall. Only time will tell. But until then, I will never stop bringing music to inmates and kids at risk.

January 19, 1999

This is the first night in awhile that the moon is shining, not a cloud in the sky. This place still gives me the creeps. The vibe in the Q is always keep on your toes. Never let your guard down. The time factor would kill me. Some men do not mind being locked up or just waiting for their time to be paroled. It's no big deal. Sooner or later the smell of freedom will happen.

This time the officer gives me a thing that the staff calls "a panic button." It kind of looks like a TV remote control only bigger. It is a gray color with red buttons on it. If someone feels like his life is in real danger, all he has to do is push this little red button and boom! All hell breaks loose. Officers come running to help you. I'm not sure if I am happy or not about being given the panic button. I feel like if I need to use the button, then I do not want to come in and teach class. As I'm walking away, another officer tells me with a grin, "If the button doesn't work, try yelling or better yet, start blowing your whistle. Someone will be right there to help you." Well, that's a real comfortable feeling knowing the officers will get to me. I just have to wait until they hear me.

As I open up the door to the Education Room, I am tapped on my left shoulder by one of my students: "What songs are you teaching us tonight Buzzy?" My reply is a couple of Rolling Stones songs, "Jumpin' Jack Flash" and "Under My Thumb."

I only have four students in class tonight. Some inmates are on lock down, while others are making their monthly phone call to their families. All four students need new strings put on their guitars, so after an hour of taking off old stinky rusted strings and then putting on four sets of new strings, we can start to learn the two new Rolling Stones songs. I must say, the inmates in my class have gotten a lot better in just a couple of weeks. One of my students asks if he can keep his old strings. Before I have a chance to say no, the other three inmates ask if they can keep their old strings, too. Well, you can imagine the danger of having some of these inmates running around with old rusted strings in a prison. It could get someone killed. I've been told that most of the inmates in prison get their tattoos from broken guitar strings dipped in ink. So, of course, my reply to my student is, "Sorry, no can do. But thanks for asking." And I begin to teach "Under My Thumb" and "Jumpin' Jack Flash."

At 8:45 p.m. sharp two officers came into the Education Room to watch. I can feel my students shy up, like four little boys. I can also tell that my students do not want me to leave tonight or to stop this music class. They are just starting to get good as a group and now it's ending next week. I have built up this class into a bunch of really strong guitar players in twelve sessions and now to tell my students goodbye, see ya next time, is sad. They all look like little kids with tears in their eyes.

I feel bad that this music class is ending but I'm overjoyed that I have been given the go-ahead to start another class in a place called H-Unit. If you have ever felt like your life is not worth living, just come and stay at the Q for a couple of hours and all those problems will go away fast. One of the officers asks me if we could play a song for them before class ends. I say, "It's up to my students." "Do you guys feel up to it?" Everyone nods their heads yes, so for the next five minutes we play and sing "Jumpin' Jack Flash." Before long those officers join in singing with us. It is my first time seeing both inmates and officers smiling, singing and being in the same room with each other without a strange vibe floating around in the air. When the song is over, both officers thank the class and me. As the door closes behind them, one of my students stands up and says, "Fuck those assholes; they sing like a couple of little girls. Buzzy, thanks again for coming in here and showing us cons how to boogie down on music. You're okay with all of us." And the class ends for the night.

As I walk out through the prison courtyard I can't help but think of what has just taken place tonight. By the time that I get to my truck I think I am going to pass out. That is how emotional my body gets when the adrenaline rush kicks in. Well, next Tuesday is my last class in the North Block. Then onto the next twelve weeks at H-Unit. What will next week bring?

January 26, 1999

This is my last class with these inmates in the main unit. My next class will be held in H-Unit. I have heard some sick stories about the inmates locked up in H-Unit. Over the weekend I bought a big referee whistle. It's so loud most of the dogs on my block bark for five minutes after I stop blowing it. The whistle given to me by the prison staff was old, rusty and didn't really work. I hope I never have to blow this whistle because if I'm blowing it I am in really big trouble. The last four months of my life teaching this class almost feels like a lifetime. But it has only been twelve weeks. It's cold and raining again tonight which sets the tone of what this prison is like to live in.

I shook my head when I heard a fourteen-year-old boy in Juvenile Hall tell me, "Buzzy, I can't wait until I can go kick it with my home boys in the Q. I wish I could go now. It's going to be cool. You don't understand. No one's going to fuck with me. I'll be protected. My homies got my back covered."

My reply to him was simple. "Son, take care of yourself and get ready to be turned into a prison bitch. I hope you like old cons sucking on your face. Because it is coming. God be with you."

As I walk to the officer's post to get my inmate movement sheet, I begin to wonder what lies ahead for me in H-Unit and also how my class is going to act, knowing it's the last night of music with them for a while.

Once I have arrived at the Education Room, I'm greeted by ten smiling inmates, all waiting with their guitars, standing under a ledge by the door trying to stay dry and warm without much luck. As I open the door, one by one the class comes together, a little wet but still all together for one last time. Tonight's song is Eric Clapton's "Before You Accuse Me Take a Look at Yourself" and then I recap everything we have played in the last twelve weeks. All in all, the night goes very smoothly. Everyone has a good time playing their guitars and singing songs.

As the class comes to a close, one of the students stands up and says, "Buzzy, we made you a thank you card but don't start crying on us and don't get mushy or huggy. Remember where you are; it's San Quentin Prison, okay." The card reads, "Buzzy thank you for putting music back in our souls. We're going to miss you a lot; signed all your prison students." Everyone signed it. As all the inmates are making jokes about life in the Q, I feel sad for them; at least I can leave.

One by one, I am given either a handshake or a big bear hug. It's very moving for all of us. Once the inmates have left, I pick up my paperwork and put away my guitar and the card the inmates have made for me as a going away gift. As I open up the door to leave, I'm greeted by the biggest, baddest looking inmate in my class. This inmate stands six foot six, weighs about two-fifty, is black with a bald head and never smiled in class, not once. But now he is smiling at me. Almost grinning. He says, "Buzzy, I have to ask you something. Did you know that most of us in your music class are lifers? Did you know that or is this the first time you're finding out about us?"

I say, "No one tells me how long you are here or why you are here, nor do I care. It's my job to teach music to inmates. I love coming here to the Q and teaching guitar." The inmate says, "Thanks again for giving us the gift of music." He also tells me to take care of myself at H-Unit and never close my eyes because it's a dangerous place. As we both walk away, I can't look back. Driving away tonight I think of everything that has happened to me here at

San Quentin. In the last twelve sessions there have been three lock downs, two executions, and a couple of gang fights. I pray the kids in Juvenile Hall never see the inside of San Quentin. It will crush their souls within hours of entering the prison. Next week a new class in H-Unit. I wonder what is around the corner and if I really want to know.

Twelve Weeks in H-Unit:
A Wild Ride

February 9, 1999

I have had a few weeks off due to paperwork and switching class from the North Block to H-Unit. But now everything is in place. Plus my prison green card has arrived so I can come and go by myself.

H-Unit looks fucking crazy. It's the Land of Lunatics. These are inmates who have served out most of their time already and only have two or three years left. H-Unit looks like a really big dog cage with lots and lots of barbwire to keep everyone in. I think, "This is going to be a wild ride." It floors me how big this prison is and what a symbol of lost hope it is. When I first enter the backside of the Q, I see a bunch of old brick buildings and factories. And, of course, razor-sharp barbwire fencing and officers with guns everywhere. I have been told the Q is one of the oldest prisons in the United States. I have also been told San Quentin houses about six thousand inmates plus five hundred sitting on Death Row.

The Q has its own electric power, water, everything; it is self-contained. If the Q loses power, it has its own generator. It is a City of Denim. From the parking lot, H-Unit looks huge. The prison dorms are made out of brick and aluminum with about one hundred and fifty inmates to a building. Most of the staff calls H-Unit Camp Quentin. H-Unit has five checkpoints that everyone has to go through in order to be let in or out. Mind you, that is after being cleared from the east gate entrance. H-Unit looks very intense with officers at their posts holding guns, while they are walking back and forth. I can hear the guard dogs barking in the background.

As I get closer I can see inmates playing basketball, working out, or just hanging out talking. I'm getting a feeling in my gut like I am about ready to be eaten by a bunch of wild dogs in a great big cage.

The contrast with the backside of San Quentin is stunning. Staff houses line the hillside with their great 1950's retro look. Kids and dogs are running up and down the streets of the prison grounds. What a way of life growing up in the shadow of San Quentin Prison. Watching baseball games being played by the inmates on the weekend from your front porch. Hoping no inmates will get mad and try to kill another inmate over a bad call from the other team. Or, wondering if someone will try to hit another inmate with a baseball bat over something stupid. What a place to bring up kids. How about when someone asks, "Where do you live?" What a shock your friends are in for when you ask, "Do you want to come over for lunch? The view of the Bay from my front porch is great, postcard perfect."

I get asked a lot, "Am I afraid of any inmates fucking with me while working in the prison?" My reply has always been, "When one is dealing with a wild pack of dogs and they show you their teeth and bark a lot, you can't show any fear back. Be strong; show lots of respect. If you do not fuck with them, chances are, they will not bite you; get the picture?"

As I arrive at the first checkpoint of H-Unit, I'm greeted by two big officers, one black and the other white. They check my guitar case, check me out and then clear me. One of the officers asks me if I had the whistle with me because from now on it's going to be my bodyguard and best friend while teaching music here at H-Unit. As I'm filling out all the paperwork, the officer behind the desk says to me with a grin on his face, "Hope you have a safe night in your music class. Keep your eyes open and good luck, son." Boy that makes me feel like dancing. As I enter the inside of H-Unit I have to walk by ten inmates standing in a line waiting to use the prison phone for their monthly call home. I notice a couple of cute black "ladies" standing there in the line talking to each other but checking me out. As I get closer, I begin wondering what in the hell were these ladies doing in H-Unit? Then it hit me. Hello! They are not ladies. They are inmates that look and act like women. One of them blows me a kiss. And says, "Hey pretty boy, show me your guitar. Maybe you could sing us a love song." My first real dose of prison life in H-Unit and I have only been here three minutes. As I reach the main yard at H-Unit a big white bad-looking tattooed inmate yells from across the yard at me, "Hey Peter Frampton, play us a song; 'Show Us The Way', rock-n-roll boss, party on," as he gives me two thumbs up.

Before I can catch my breath, two Arabic-looking inmates wearing turbans approach the two officers, chanting something about Mohammed and me. They are trying to tell the officers and me what we should be doing to change our lives. Hello? Who's in prison?

Once I arrive at the officers' main post inside H-Unit I feel a little better. But not much. Every inmate in H-Unit is giving me a look, like I have just dropped in from another land. The main officer on night duty introduces himself and tells me that he is getting ready to retire in a few weeks. He is moving to Florida and really looking forward to leaving this shit hole of a place. He tells me that he has been working here at the prison for about fifteen long hard years and has seen his share of unhappy times. With a big laugh he says, "Fifteen years is a long time to work anywhere; but add in San Quentin Prison to the list, it will make any man go mad. I kid you not."

I can't really blame the man; fifteen years of working in a prison would make anyone nuts. The officer tells me I must be a ballsy guy because no one has ever done a music program here at H-Unit. This is the very first time. "Good luck; because you're going to need it." Because it's a new class, all the staff at H-Unit are a little jumpy and nervous. The class will be held in the officers' conference room that is used for all the staff meetings. As I'm talking to an officer I hear, "music class will begin in ten minutes," blasted over the speakers. "Well, good luck tonight," the officer, says. If anything happens just use your whistle or start yelling. Someone will help you." So here I am in H-Unit waiting for my students to show up for class.

One by one, inmates start coming into the hall, lining up so they can be given the okay to go to class with me. The office complex in H-Unit feels cold and sterile and smells really clean, like the strong scent of Pinesol. The lighting overhead is bright and it gives off a mild hum. The floors are the cleanest I have ever seen.

I end up having eight students. A couple of the white inmates look like pirates to me. One is missing his front four teeth and the other is wearing a black patch over his right eye. Both inmates have loads of tattoos all over their bodies. The Mexican inmates all look pretty young except for one student. He has to be about sixty years old and never smiles. These inmates in H-Unit seem much more intimidating than the inmates on the North Block. They have a "fuck you" attitude. The inmates in H-Unit will eventually be released, unlike the inmates on the North Block. I think that is where the attitude comes from.

Once inside the conference room, the inmates are told to behave themselves or else. I wonder what the hell "or else" means. The officer then locks the door, telling me that he will be back in two hours. "Good luck" the officer says as he is walking away.

Everyone is telling me good luck. That is all I have been hearing for the last half an hour. After the officer leaves the room, one of the inmates looks at me and says, "I play the guitar five hours a day, seven days a week. I want to learn to play the blues. Can you show me some blues, boss?"

"Sure," I say. "No problem. Do you sing?" I ask each inmate about his experience singing and playing the guitar. About half the class knows something about music; the others just want to learn anything they can. Every inmate's guitar needs strings put on. So after thirty minutes of unwinding and winding strings, the class is ready to rock. As I teach these inmates their first song, Bob Seger's "Old Time Rock-n-Roll" I can feel a very heavy vibe in the air. No one is smiling. So I say, "Who can sing this song? I would like to have one of you sing the song. Who is it going to be?"

That breaks the ice. Two inmates look up at me, smiling like sweet little boys being given the gift of a big bag of candy. A black inmate with arms the size of my legs smiles at me and asks, "Can I sing first? Is that possible, boss?" Now another inmate says, "I've never sang before, but if it's okay with the other students, I'd like to give it a try after Marvin Gaye. What do ya think, can we go through the song a couple of times or what?"

After three times of going through the Seger song, it begins to take shape. I have each student sing a verse and then everyone sings the chorus. Just then, yet another inmate tells me he plays the bass guitar. Without saying another word, he picks up his guitar and starts thumping out bass lines on the first two strings of his guitar. We all sit there listening to this black inmate with our mouths hanging open while he plays the bass lines to the Tower of Power song "What Is Hip," note for note.

My first thought is I would like to be in a band with this guy. He lays down a mean, heavy groove. The problem is he is an inmate in San Quentin Prison and did not get here by being a nice fellow that's for sure. At 8:45 the officer comes back to the conference room, unlocks the door and announces, "The party's over for tonight. Wrap it up; get your paperwork, guitar and butts in gear. Bed Count is in fifteen minutes." With a big sigh of relief, I say, "Great job tonight, gentlemen. Remember to practice." At that point I feel a little better about my new class and a little sad about my old classmates at the North Block. I kind of miss those guys.

I'm starting to feel and see the subculture of the inmate's way of life here in the different sections of the Q. It's sinking in fast at H-Unit. It's in the air everyone breathes; it's also in the ground that we walk on, the feeling of deep despair that will never go away. There is too much pain in this place. It is the land of broken dreams and lonely hearts.

I decide to not wait for an escort tonight. I think I can walk back to the officer's main post by myself. The two-minute walk across the main yard feels like it's taking ten hours or more. I'm scared shitless walking alongside all those bad ass looking inmates.

I want to throw up or run. But know I can't do either. Catcalls, inmates blowing me kisses, it's a sick and creepy lifestyle. Once I get back to the officer's main post to be checked out, I'm shaking from head to toe and my shirt is drenched with sweat. But I am alive. Hallelujah! I will never be that stupid ever again to walk alone through the prison yard at H-Unit without officers on each side of me. What the hell was I thinking? I must be crazy.

These inmates at H-Unit have their own style of talking: everything in prison is slang. They have their own code of living and dying. As far as crime in prison goes, it happens all the time; you just have to wait until it's your turn. As I'm walking to my truck I notice a place the staff and the inmates call "The Ranch." All inmates at the Ranch can walk around pretty freely. There are no bars, no cells, and no barbwire fencing. But, yes, those officers in the guard towers are always watching. Their guns are always ready to shoot. The inmates at the Ranch just can't cross the yellow dotted line. Only staff can. With five lookout posts, none of these inmates can run far.

Driving home I remember those two black inmates who looked like cute ladies blowing kisses at me with their high cheekbones and their long fingernails. Their breast size had to be at least a "C" cup. They were even dressed like women. Their prison shirts were tied to show cleavage. I was told by one of the officers that those inmates are called "sugar shorts" by the other inmates. It's way too strange for my mind to comprehend. And to think some of the kids I'm working with in Juvenile Hall can't wait to end up living here.

These kids keep telling me that I don't understand. They will be okay, no one is going to hurt or fuck with them; they will be kicking it with their home boys; they will be safe; it's okay, do not worry. The truth is it will make them grow up really fast and very old all at the same time. Have it, live your life as an inmate locked up in San Quentin Prison. Just remember one thing: Never sleep with both eyes shut, never.

February 23, 1999

This is my second time coming into the H-Unit. Last week blew my mind. For days I thought about those two black inmates I thought were ladies. I hope I can make it through all twelve classes at H-Unit without getting too freaked out over things like inmates blowing me kisses or giving me the prison glare to see if I will cry.

H-Unit is the creepiest place I have ever been. I thought the North Block had a dark vibe, but that was not anything close to H-Unit. In a strange way, life in H-Unit is like a breeding ground for lost souls.

I always park my truck alongside the curb right next to the prison visitors' bathrooms. I put my truck in park, lock it up, walk the five steps to the bathroom, use it, then walk quickly back to my truck before an officer can yell at me for parking in the red. Anyhow, enough said. So I always stop, park and pee before going in.

Inmates in prison always have eyes on them: watching them eat, taking showers, going to the bathroom, talking, sleeping whatever an inmate does while in prison is being monitored through another person's eyes, always. There is no privacy in San Quentin, none whatsoever.

I remind myself to ask for an officer's escort in and out of H-Unit from now on.

I will never walk unescorted in the H-Unit main yard again. Too many looks of "fuck you" or looks like "I want to fuck you" on the inmates' faces.

I can hear the words blasting from the speakers outside in H-Unit, "music class will begin in ten minutes; the Guitar Man is here." When I ask for an escort, I see two inmates waiting to be transferred back to the main prison block. These inmates look mean and very ugly, never smiling once. They just sit there looking right through me like I'm not there. I don't know what kind of food they feed these inmates because both smell pretty sick. Almost like cow shit or milk gone bad, plus the unpleasant stink of underarm odor fills the room.

When my officer escort shows up to take me to class; the first thing I ask him is, "What is up with those inmates sitting in the office? And why do they stink so bad?" With a little laugh he explains to me, "That's the smell of prison. Every inmate in here stinks; it's just how it is, son. And as for why those inmates are waiting in the office, who knows? It could be anything from paperwork to going back up to the North Block. Who cares? This place is a fucking mad house."

As I'm being escorted across the main yard in H-Unit, I notice a lot of the inmates playing basketball, working out, talking to each other or just waiting to be paroled. I have been told most inmates will return to prison within months of being released. It seems to me, life in H-Unit is a lot about doing nothing except counting time and smoking cheap hand-rolled cigarettes.

As I reach the inside of the officer's post, I'm approached by three inmates waiting to get into the music class. Each inmate has a look on his face that says, please teach me how to play the guitar or I'm going to go crazy inside this shit house. I keep telling myself, nothing is going to happen to me. I just don't want to ever piss off any inmates or officers while I'm in this cage teaching. So all I can say is, "Sorry there's nothing I can do. You will have to talk to the head officer here at H-Unit. Maybe he can help you, because I can't."

As the officer unlocks the door he says, "You must be doing something right; the word's out on you and you've only been in here two times. Shit, that was fast."

With a big bang, the steel door slams shut, but I have to ask, "What do you mean the word's out on me?" He says, "Respect is everything in a prison; everything else is bullshit. But to inmates respect is the number one rule. And it looks like you got H-Unit's respect. You've got some big balls my friend. Have a safe class tonight. See ya in a couple of hours." As I wait in the hallway for my students to arrive I can't help but wonder how big of a turnover there is with prison staff. I could not work in here forty hours a week. The thought of coming into the Q everyday makes my head hurt.

My class tonight has eight students again. One of the inmates tells me he only has one year and six months left. Being locked up for the last five years has changed his life forever. He tells me prison life is like being locked away with a bunch of mean, wild and crazy fucking dogs, all living in a real big doghouse. I wonder what crimes got each of my students time in prison. Was it drugs, rape, murder, car jacking, or gang banging. There are lots of young gang bangers walking around H-Unit like sharks looking for their next kill. Some don't even look eighteen years old. After roll call, I tune all eight guitars and then show the inmates "Rock This Town" by the Stray Cats and the song "Gloria." After about an hour I had all the inmates singing, "G-L-O-R-I-A" at the top of their lungs. What a sight; what a sound.

All of the inmates seem a lot more talkative tonight, asking me questions about music and the outside world. But when I look at their faces I can see the torment of the prison lifestyle riding hard on their souls. The rule for me is never talk about anything other than music. I will talk about music for hours; but I will not answer any questions about anything else. That's my answer to all the inmates. Music, let's talk. Anything that has to do with the outside world, my family, or me forget about it. I'm going to clam up.

Some of the inmates I have been working with in the Q almost come across like mean little boys that never grew up mentally. In a sad kind of a way, I feel very grateful to be the first musician to teach music at H-Unit. I also feel it's good for me to bring in the music because music calms their restless souls. I do feel I'm making a little difference in my students' lives. God knows I am not going to make any of these inmates rock stars, but hopefully the music will mellow them out a bit.

A couple of inmates in H-Unit really give me the creeps. Some in the music class I don't trust at all. I'm keeping my eyes open. They seem to be much crazier and way more stressed out than my first class up in the North Block. These inmates have lots and lots of tattoos everywhere, arms, chest, legs, head, fingers and the neck. That neck tattoo stuff must hurt a lot. Prison tattoos are a big thing.

It is about looking macho and having power. Power is everything to all inmates in the prison. Prison tattoos are put on with pen ink and wire or guitar strings.

It must hurt like hell having another inmate poking your neck with a broken guitar string for about two hours. Needles are bad enough; but it must burn having them put on with dirty, broken guitar strings, all in the name of power and pride in prison. Go figure. At 8:45 p.m. two officers arrive to let us out. Once again a very moving night.

Not forgetting about last week and how creepy it felt to walk around H-Unit without officers by my side, I ask for an escort back out. The head officer on duty tells me to sit in a chair and wait till another officer can be called in to escort me back. "You're in no hurry, are you, son?" The officer asks me. "No, I have all the time in the world. I'll just sit in this chair and wait; thanks," I say.

After what seems like a lifetime of waiting, the main door to the office flies open and the bald head of a really big black officer pops in. His head turns real slow, looking all around the room till he spots me sitting there in the chair. He turns even slower, looking me straight in the eyes and says with a half grin, "Are you going my way? What's the matter; can't you take the freak show? Welcome to the inmates circus, H-Unit, San Quentin State Prison." Before I can respond he adds, "At any given moment, there can be up to one thousand inmates walking around the main grounds of H-Unit. And with only twelve officers on duty inside H-Unit and given the fact of all the blind spots, the potential for danger is pretty high; wouldn't ya say?" All I can say is, "When do we leave?" That officer stands straight up and booms "Let's ride my friend; the bus is leaving."

As we walk back to the other officers' post, my escort tells me "Once most of these inmates at H-Unit get back out on the streets, it will only take three, maybe four, weeks before they will re-offend. Inmates always come back to their home away from home. That is how it has been for a long, long time. You are not going to change these inmates, nor am I. Once one of these little gang banger bastards gets his ass inside the walls of the Q, he is no longer a person. They have now become just a number with no future."

As I arrive at the officers' post, I thank my escort and say, "Be safe and have a good night." What would make a young boy want to grow up in a place like this, always looking over his shoulder, or having some old crusty con drooling on his back as he is sucking your neck? I can't see what is so cool and macho about living in the land of doom. Once you have seen the inside of a prison and lived the life of an inmate, your soul will be tainted forever.

H-Unit is a zoo. I have only been in here twice and it's already blowing me away; but I still have ten more classes left on my contract. The things that go on behind the walls in a prison are sometimes not even close to human. That's when the animal instinct kicks in. Survival of the fittest. What will happen next week?

March 9, 1999

It's my third time coming into H-Unit and my fifteenth time coming into San Quentin State Prison. As I drive up to the east gate entrance of the prison to use the restroom, I notice a long line of visitors waiting to be cleared so they can go into the prison. Many are from churches, others from NA or AA. A lot of people from the outside come to San Quentin to help the inmates in one way or another. So I have to wait for fifteen minutes to get cleared. Then I drive around the back side of the Q. I can smell the prison stench in the air. After parking my truck, I wait another ten minutes to be cleared. Like I have said, time is everything in prison. But I have to admit San Quentin Prison is a major adrenaline rush for me. It's hard-core living on the edge. I do not care how big or bad you are, if you've never been in a prison before, you are going to freak out.

As soon as I enter H-unit, I start getting catcalls from some of the inmates. Things like, "Hey pretty boy, shake that ass for all of us," or "Hey music man, what are ya doing after class is over? Can ya come over and sing me a couple of love songs?" I am starting to feel like a porkchop.

The officer on night duty tells me to use the panic button for music class tonight. He says, "If anything feels nutty tonight, just push it. It's better being safe then sorry." I go to put it in my pocket when the officer shouts, "Don't put it in your pocket! You don't want to push that sucker unless you have to. If you push that little red button all hell breaks loose; you can bet on it. The next sound you and the inmates will hear will be the sound of boots, keys, and guns. No worry, son, and by the way, all your students are here and standing in line waiting for class to begin. Have fun!"

Now I must say, those were some pretty scary words, but I do what he tells me. I take the little box and hold onto it, making sure I do not hit the little red button. The officer tells my students to be good inmates; and not to fuck around! As he shuts and locks the door, waving goodbye to us, one of the students says in a real low voice, "Hey Buzzy, don't push that button or drop it. Do you want me to hold onto it for you till this class is done?" Everyone in the room starts laughing. Boy, do I feel stupid, but I have to laugh, too.

Another inmate says, "Don't worry, boss, we're not going to fuck with you. If anything, we will be there for you if any shit happens while you're with us in H-Unit."

The songs tonight are ZZ Top's "Sharp Dressed Man" and "Burning Love" by Elvis. The inmates tell me ZZ Top and the Rolling Stones rank high when it comes to music in prison. The inmates are more then happy to help sing both songs, again singing at the top of their lungs just like last week.

I'm finding that when we play and sing as a class, most of the inmates start to smile and loosen up! It's safe for these inmates and me to have fun in music class. All Elvis songs are huge in prison too. I'm asked if I can teach everyone "Jailhouse Rock" and "Teddy Bear" sometime in the future. "Sure, I say. I'd be glad to show you guys any Elvis song. Just ask; and thank you very much!" Again everyone in the room begins laughing.

After we have played the song "Burning Love" for the seventh time, a couple of the inmates keep singing the words, "Hunka, hunka, burning love," trying their best to sound just like The King himself. My face hurts from laughing and the tears are running down my cheeks and splashing on the side of my guitar.

As I wipe my eyes, I hear the door open up. The officer barks, "Okay ladies, it's time for bed check. Ten minutes and counting. If I were you, I'd kick it in the ass. You don't want to be late. Mr. Guitar Man, your escort is waiting." They all get up fast, pack their stuff and file out of the room, asking no questions or even talking. As we walk down the hallway, no one says a word. Everyone just looks straight ahead, never smiling, only doing what they are being told to do. As I come upon the officer's post, I'm told to sit down and wait. My escort is getting a cup of coffee. As soon as I sit down, in walks the same black officer as last week. Only this time he is smiling and singing the Al Green song "Let's Stay Together." He stops singing and says to me. "Are you ready to leave because I'm your escort and my motor is running, let's buckle-up and ride."

While we walk to the out-post, he explains a little bit about H-Unit. He says, "There are a lot of macho attitudes in H-Unit because up to 80 percent of these inmates are very young, tough, and stupid, the potential for a bad explosion between inmates and gang bangers is really great. Plus, some are black or Mexican kids from poor families or white boys with bad attitudes mixing with each other all caged up like dogs. It makes for a lot of problems between races and gang members."

He asks me how I liked working with the inmates and what my wife thinks about me teaching music in a prison. I tell him, I love teaching music anywhere I can. I admit coming into H-Unit kind of gives me the creeps, but overall it seems to be fine so far. And, as for my wife, well I tell him a real short story. I had to go to an orientation last Saturday morning at the Q, only outside of the walls. So I brought my wife because she'd never seen it up close. After the class was over and everyone had said their good-byes, I shook my boss's hand and thanked her for the chance to teach music to the inmates. My wife and I decided to go to the prison gift shop where people can buy stuff that inmates make and the money goes back to help operate the prison.

As we got closer to the gift shop, I said, "Honey, I will handle everything, don't say a word. Let's just look." When I opened up the door, I could see this inmate sitting behind the glass counter. His hair was greased straight back. He had the words "Fuck You" tattooed on his neck and he was reading a book. When the door shut behind us with a bang, the inmate never moved or looked up. I could hear music coming from the back room. As my wife and I walked around looking at the cool stuff the inmates had made, my eyes met his. The first thing out of my mouth was, "So, how are you doing this fine morning?" His only reply was, "It's Groundhog Day, boss." I thought to myself, what the fuck is he talking about. So I said one more time, "Nice day outside, how ya doing?" And again, this inmate said to me, "It's just Groundhog Day." So now I looked over to my wife and said to her, "Honey, did you know that it's already Groundhog Day?" Now between that inmate and my wife giving me the same look, I knew that I had said something very stupid. Without saying a word, my wife just moved her lips, telling me to shut up.

After buying a couple of things, we left. Walking back to the truck, my wife explained to me that Groundhog Day is a movie about a guy played by Bill Murray and it's the same thing every day, nothing ever changes. Right before I opened up the door for her she said to me, "Honey, by the way Groundhog Day was last month. I would have told you that, but you told me to keep my mouth shut. You would handle everything, remember?"

So my answer to my escort is, "My wife is very cool and understanding about me coming into the Q as long as I come home every time."

March 16, 1999

Driving to the prison tonight I keep telling myself to just keep calm. Because the last few times coming into H-Unit has freaked me out way too much. As I walk into the prison I can feel that same ugly vibe of hopelessness in the air. A kind of kaleidoscope of grays, where a man's dignity is all but gone. As I pass the Ranch, I can hear some inmates yelling, "Hey, pretty boy, rock-n-roll for all of us here in Quentin."

Three officers are waiting to escort me to my class. When I ask why there are three officers, I am told H-Unit had a lot of shit going down between inmates in the last three or four days, so the staff felt it would be a lot safer for me to have two more officers, just in case. These are the times I begin to wonder what the hell I'm doing working in a prison! Being escorted to my class has its ups and downs. The up is I feel a little bit safer, but not much. The down side has to be having one thousand inmates watching me being walked through the main yard like fresh meat being prepared for tonight's dinner. Some of the inmates grab themselves while drooling or worse yet, yell things like, "Welcome to our city of hell, rock star." And all I am trying to do is just teach a little music to these inmates.

As I wait for my students, I look out the office windows at the inmates in H-Unit walking around like zombies. The sight of old cons with no teeth and lots of tattoos kissing on another inmate's neck makes the hair on my back stand up. Thank God I'm locked inside with officers. The hardest part of working at H-Unit is walking in or out of the place. It's just crazy, there's no getting around it. Tonight's class only has five inmates, very small. One inmate is sick and two others were released a few days ago.

I show all five students the songs "Sharp Dressed Man" and "Tush," both by ZZ Top. They all sing and laugh while playing the songs. Two of the inmates know every single word to both songs. The three hours just blow by way too fast for all of us. Right before 9:00 p.m. one of my students asks me, "Hey Buzzy, why don't you stay just a bit longer tonight, so we can all play some more music with each other? What do ya think, boss, is that possible?" I tell him that I would love to stay, but I have really got to be going. It's 9:00 p.m. straight up. Bed count is in ten minutes.

Another inmate looks at me and says in a real low voice, "Hey, Buzzy, we've got an extra bed, some clean sheets, you can stay overnight here if you want to." I smile and ask, "Great! What's on TV?" Another inmate adds, "If you stay overnight here in H-Unit at San Quentin Prison tonight, then Buzzy, you'll be on TV." That puts a smile on everyone's face. We all laugh as the officers unlock the door. As the last inmate leaves, he says, "Buzzy, I'm so happy. I just found out today that I only have eighteen months left in prison before I can smell freedom again. Isn't that cool. Ten years in this hell hole always looking over my shoulder, never having a good night's sleep, wondering when I'm going to get beat up or gang raped, that's a fucked up life let me tell ya. When I get out this time, I'm never coming back. This is the last time that I ever want to see the inside of a prison. See ya next week, boss. Be safe."

An officer points his finger at me, grins and says, "Okay Guitar Man. It's time to go home. Your escort's waiting by the officers' post, unless you want to stay overnight." My reply to the officer is, "No, I'm ready to go. It's an OK place to visit, but I wouldn't want to live here, let alone stay overnight or sleep here."

As I walk back across the main yard, I'm surprised at how calm everything feels. Nighttime seems to bring on peacefulness to the air. Plus every inmate in the Q is locked down for bed count. The School of Hard Knocks, where some men are broken like horses. And all of the bad stories that we are told about San Quentin Prison are indeed very real and true. I hope that when I get home tonight I can sleep.

March 23, 1999

It's real cold and foggy. Winter is in full swing on the west coast. As I drive my truck up to the east gate entrance of the prison, I can see about ten people waiting to be cleared. A lot of Bay Area church congregations come into San Quentin to sing, volunteer to read or counsel the inmates. Everyone has his or her own reasons for coming into the prison. For me it's the music. I know it means everything to the inmates who have been locked up for a long time. This is the part of life that your mother warned you about. There is a man that I see every Tuesday night standing in line carrying a Bible. He has been coming into the prison to pray with the inmates for the last seven years. God bless him for bringing in a little comfort. I have never met him, but I have heard the inmates talk about him. I wonder if there are any stories starting to float around the Q about me yet?

Ironically, tonight one of the officers says, "You must be the Guitar Man everyone has been talking about. The inmates in H-Unit seem to respect you, my friend. That's good! I'm your escort tonight, so sign in and we're good to go."

Over the prison speakers I hear, "Music class will begin in ten minutes. The Guitar Man is now in the house." Great, I think, now all one thousand inmates in H-Unit know I'm here teaching music or walking in the main yard. I think if I am ever caught in the middle of a lock down, my best bet is to drop down to my knees shouting at the top of my lungs, "Please don't shoot me, I'm the Guitar Man." Only twenty officers on duty at H-Unit watching over one thousand inmates at all times makes for a really crazy working vibe.

I teach my students the songs "Peaceful Easy Feeling" and "Runaway." "Runaway" sounds great; everyone picks up the song fast. Two students, who know every word, even take turns singing the song. It feels wonderful that the class is working together, plus the inmates are learning a lot about self-esteem, pride, working as a team, and music. Things they should have been taught as children growing up, not as grown men living out their lives behind bars.

At 8:45 p.m. an officer unlocks the door and tells us, "The class is over. It's time to go to bed." As the room is cleared out the inmates go back to their world and I go back to mine. I'm always reminded in H-Unit of who's in charge. What a dark, cold feeling to live within prison; who is the boss this week of your life?

Driving home tonight I keep thinking of the kids at Juvenile Hall that I'll be working with tomorrow morning. How many of them will end up in San Quentin or some other penitentiary. If I can keep one child out of prison by talking to him about what it's like being in San Quentin, then I'm saving a kid's soul and life. Kids labeled "at risk" stand a good chance of ending up living on the streets or going to prison or worse, dead. At least everyone in music class keeps smiling; that is a good sign.

March 30, 1999

It's much easier to come into the Q when it is cold, foggy, and raining because it sets the tone of the prison. Being locked up in a cage while birds are flying and singing all around me as I watch the sunset on the bay from behind bars is very strange. At these times, freedom is so close I can see it; but it's just out of reach.

In spite of everything, I have loved every strange moment in prison teaching the inmates music; even the creepy stories that make my skin crawl. I take it all in and, afterwards, sit in my truck and record what happened in class on a cassette tape player, so I will not forget.

As I pull into the prison staff parking lot I see another baseball game being played at the Ranch. Everyone is having a great time laughing, joking, and just having fun, except for the officers on duty walking the grounds of the prison, or the officers in the guard towers carrying guns watching the inmates.

As I walk past some of the inmates watching the ball game they start cat calling me, saying things like, "Hey Ringo, can you sing us any Beatle songs," or "Where's the rest of the band?" Here's a good one, "Do you take requests? Can we hear the song 'Free Bird?'" I never make eye contact with any inmates outside of my music class. I just look straight ahead and keep on walking. As I'm halfway to H-Unit's main gates, it begins to rain really hard. Now remember, no one can run in a prison. It's one of the biggest rules, even if you are getting soaked to the bone. No running or even walking fast.

So by the time that I arrive at H-Unit's officers' post, I'm soaking wet and with no other pants or shirt to put on. I can see that it might be a long night in music class.

As I wait for an escort I can feel blood rushing through my body and my heart starting to pump a little faster. I get this feeling every time I enter H-Unit. I don't think that I will ever get used to being locked up in H-Unit.

When I reach the officers' main post I drop off my guitar inside the office so that I can get a cup of coffee. I whisper to the officer who is talking on the phone, "I'll be right back. I'm going to get myself a cup of coffee." When I come back to the office to pick up my guitar, the officer in charge starts barking at me in a real soft growling voice. "Don't you ever do that again, son. Don't you ever just walk into my office while I'm on the phone without knocking! Do you understand me, boy?" All I can muster out of my mouth is, "Yes sir; I'm sorry." At that moment, I feel like an inmate myself.

Boy, do I hate being treated like a dog and being yelled at. It makes me feel like shit. I must have apologized to that officer about one thousand times in less than a minute. His reply is simply, "Welcome to H-Unit and the pressure of working in a prison."

Once all my students show up for class we are escorted to the back office and locked inside the room for the next two and one-half hours. The songs tonight are "Sea of Love" and an Elvis song called "Little Sister." I have ten inmates tonight and everyone loves the songs. Four inmates ask if they can take turns singing "Sea of Love." What a sight.

About 8:00 p.m. one of my students stops playing his guitar and yells, "Stop playing ladies; I've got something to say to Buzzy. Buzzy, I've been in and out of prisons all of my life. I had been slamming PCP and robbing people at knifepoint and that's what landed me here in San Quentin. I wish I had known you before I fucked up my life. Maybe because of music I could have been saved. So, thank you for coming into this fucked up place just to show a few cons the gift of music. You're one hell of a person." Then he asks me if he can sing the class a few country songs that he has just learned.

I say that would be cool; give it to us. So for the next ten minutes that inmate sings and plays songs by Johnny Cash, George Jones, Hank Williams and Merle Haggard.

We all sit there watching him with our mouths hanging open. I am always amazed at how much talent there is in San Quentin Prison. Some inmates draw, paint, write stories or poems, and a lot of inmates play music. Most of these inmates discovered their gift after being locked up. What a shame to waste time being locked up when you have so much to offer the world. Teaching a music class in prison is a spiritual experience of sheer human emotion that hits me right in my gut. It makes me cry inside because it's raw living behind the walls of San Quentin, closed off from the rest of the free world.

At about 8:00 p.m. the prison coffee that I drank earlier kicks in. I talk as fast as I can without falling over my words. I get hot and then cold. It feels like I'm on a high-octane fuel ride. My body is running about one thousand miles a minute. My heart is screaming, "No more prison coffee." But, what can I do? It's way too late to turn back. I'm grinding my teeth together. My legs are shaking and I can't sit still. All of this over one cup of coffee. Just then an inmate asks me if I ever smoke cigars and would I like one? I answer, "Yes; but why do you ask?" The next thing I know I'm being given a Swisher Sweet cigar and a smile from this inmate.

My first thought is where in the hell did this inmate get the cigar and should I be taking it from him? I still have to keep telling myself that I'm teaching music in a state prison and these inmates are put in here for a reason. As the class comes to a close, I thank all my students for making the music class easy tonight.

When the officer on duty unlocks the door, I have to ask him when the staff coffee was made. He looks at me and asks, "You didn't drink any of that shit did you? We always make the coffee the night before; so it sits in the pot cooking all night and day. By the time the night crew shows up for work, start your engines baby!"

"Did you drink some of our liquid crank, my friend?" I tell him, "Yes, I did and I will never do that again. Being tweaked in prison is not a very good thing for me. I hope no inmates ever drink that coffee. I always thought bar coffee was the strongest stuff in the world. Boy, was I wrong. I will never ever drink prison staff coffee again." Driving home I think about that inmate who sang the country songs to everyone. What a strange environment H-Unit is!

April 13, 1999

This is my first night back in music class at H-Unit in two weeks. I have been on vacation in Mexico with my wife getting a much-needed rest. While we were away, I had a lot of time to think about San Quentin and Juvenile Hall, and how much it means to the inmates and kids at risk to have the exposure to music once a week. I hope no one asks me why I am so tan or where have I been for two weeks because I will feel really guilty telling my students how much fun I had hanging out on the beach in Mexico.

Driving into the staff parking lot seems a little easier tonight. Who knows why. Maybe having some time away helped settle me down. Walking past the Ranch I am sure that some inmate will yell out something as usual, but tonight it doesn't happen. As I enter the front gates of H-Unit that easygoing feeling goes away, fast. As soon as my escort starts walking me across the main yard in H-Unit I begin freaking out. My heart is pumping so hard I think it will burst. My hands are cold and I am damn sure I'll pass out at any moment. But, by the time I reach the officers' main post I pull myself together. After signing my name into the logbook, four inmates and I are escorted into the back office and locked in.

After the officer leaves us alone, the inmates start talking shit about the prison staff. Thank God no inmate asks me about my tan or where I have been for the last two weeks. I teach my class the songs "Woolly Bully" and the ZZ Top song "Tush." About an hour into the class, one of the inmates starts laughing really hard, almost to the point of crying. Then he starts clapping his hands together. Everyone in the room stops playing their guitars and one of the other inmates asks him, "Are you fucking nuts, Alice, what's going on in your mind?" With that said, that inmate grins and then shouts out the words, "Look out world because here I come again. I'm being paroled in three days. Hide all the girls. After being locked up for five years, I've got some catching up to do." All of the inmates in the room began laughing and giving each other high fives. All I can think is "Oh my God, let me out of here. I want to run home and throw up." There are very few words that can explain what goes on in prison. It's extremely painful and raw for me seeing inmates joking around with each other about raping little girls and then laughing about it. Just then, another inmate tells me he is getting paroled tomorrow; but not to worry that he will be seeing me the next time he is in San Quentin. Then he smiles at me as he says, "Only kidding, Buzzy, it's a little prison humor. I'm just fucking with your mind. Sorry about that, boss!"

I have been doing this prison music program at San Quentin for seven months now; but it almost feels like a lifetime ago when I first entered the main gates of the prison. All in all, the class is very mellow tonight.

As the officer comes back to unlock the door I thank all of my students for a job well done in class tonight. On the way out, one of the officers standing next to the door waves me over to him saying, "I'm your escort back out of H-Unit. Are you ready to leave"? I nod yes and off we go. While we walk back across H-Unit's main yard, the officer asks me what I think about the whole prison lifestyle here in Quentin. Before I have a chance to answer him, he says to me, "Did you know that 85 percent of the inmates in H-Unit are locked up for being sex offenders"? As we reach the drop off point for me, I turn to my officer escort and say to him, "I love music. I think prison is the strangest place that I have ever been. The lifestyle in prison is something from another land and, no, I didn't know that there are so many sex offenders locked up in H-Unit. That makes me sick!"

On the way home, my head begins to pound and my heart cries thinking about how messed up the world has become.

April 20, 1999

Driving to San Quentin I've been hearing reports over the radio about a school shooting somewhere in Colorado. One of the reporters says he has heard there might be up to fifteen students dead, possibly killed by two other boys, classmates with a death wish.

The reporter goes on to say these two kids just walked into the school and opened fire, shooting everyone in sight, in some cases toying with some of the kids before shooting them. Before I turn off the radio another news flash says both boys were found dead inside the school. They shot each other at the same time. I turn off the radio, and walk to H-Unit thinking about kids killing kids and again what this world has come to.

My heart aches for the kids in today's world. As I wait for my escort, I ask the officer on night duty if he had heard anything about a school shooting in Colorado? His reply is, "No, son, I've been working inside H-Unit for about three hours now; haven't heard a thing about any school shootings, sorry."

Once again I get that crampy feeling right in the middle of my gut, plus the hot flashes. Thank God, I don't feel like passing out. All of this going on inside of my head while walking around in a prison. My escort unlocks the door and says, "Have a good class. Be safe and don't let your guard down!" I say, "No worries. I'll see ya in two and a half hours. Thanks for the escort."

As I wait for the rest of my students to show up for class I think about the kids that have been killed in Colorado. I only have five inmates for music class and by the time class starts, it's already 7:00 p.m. So for the next two hours I teach my students the songs "Johnny B. Goode," "Hound Dog" and "Blue Suede Shoes."

Everything runs smoothly. No badmouthing staff, no messing with my mind. Everyone just rocks out to the music. Once again at 9:00 p.m. an officer comes to the room, unlocks the door and tells us it's time to go.

Back in my truck, I turn on my radio and hear the words Columbine High School murders. I cry most of the way home. It makes me sad to see kids killing kids just for the fun of it. To do bad stuff to someone else, push life to the limit, and then jump over the edge, like there is no tomorrow breaks my heart. This is truly a sad day for the kids of Columbine and a much sadder day for all of the kids around the world.

May 11, 1999

I missed the last two Tuesday night music classes in H-Unit because of an execution. The prison always puts all of the inmates on lock-down, which means no inmates leave their cell for up to twenty-four hours or longer. Most of the inmates that enter the Q already have very long criminal records. Things like rape, arson, murder or anything else that you can think of. So being locked up for long periods of time is no big deal for a lot of these inmates.

Tonight is my seventeenth time in San Quentin. I'm proud of the fact that I have made it through all seventeen classes without any shit happening to me, no bad juju yet. As I walked up to the main gates, I get a cold chill thinking that just days ago, some inmate was put to death.

As I enter the officers' post I'm again greeted by the old southern officer with a real thick good ol' boy accent. He says to me with a slow southern voice, "You all have to sign your name into the prison log book. I have already called for your escort and he should be here in about three minutes or less." Then he picks up a small microphone, presses a big red button on the desk and says, "The Guitar Man is here. The music class will begin in about ten minutes." He turns off the prison microphone and says, "There you go, boy. They're all waiting for ya. Don't have too much fun tonight; otherwise we may have to keep ya overnight!"

My escorts are two big officers, one black and one white. Both really buffed out and extremely mean-looking. Neither one of them smiles or says a single word to me. The black officer looks like a pro football player. Maybe six foot, eight inches, weighing in at about three hundred pounds. As I'm being escorted across the exercise yard in H-Unit some inmate yells out, "God damn it; boys the Rolling Stones have dropped in." Another inmate shouts out, "It's the Guitar Man! Can you play "Free Bird" for us, boy?" Walking across the yard feels like it takes hours. Everything moves in slow motion for me in San Quentin. It's like a really bad dream; only this is real life happening right now.

Class tonight is small, four inmates and everyone is very low key. I teach my class the songs "King of the Road," "Your Cheatin' Heart" and "Old Man Down The Road." About ten minutes into class one of the inmates leans over my way and asks me, "Hey Buzzy, how much do you like guitars?" I say, "I love guitars, all sizes and colors. I love guitars a lot. Why?" He pulls out this book that has the whole history of the guitar. The book must be over five hundred pages. So for twenty-five minutes, the five of us look at every page, checking out every electric guitar ever made.

The Swisher Sweet inmate hands me another cigar while we are talking about Les Paul and Jimmy Page. It makes for a strange vibe when inmates try to buy my friendship. The San Quentin Prison Handbook reads, "Never take any gifts at anytime from any inmate." It's buying friendship and that is crossing some heavy lines.

Tonight is the last time I will take a cigar from him. It's creepy for me having some of these inmates trying to be my buddy. Coming into the prison and teaching music is one thing, but becoming friends with a couple of these inmates will never happen. I can do without the lifestyle these inmates have going for them. But I am glad that not one inmate brings up the word "execution," because I would not know what to say anyway. After class is over and I'm being escorted back across H-Unit's main yard, I hear a couple of inmates yelling things to me like, "Hey rock star, show us a little sugar; or hey Guitar Man, how much are music lessons? Can we work out something about the payments?"

There is nothing stranger than seeing about thirty buffed-out, tattooed, mean-looking inmates blowing kisses and laughing while giving me the finger. What a freak show. My first class at the Q seemed a little bit nicer than the inmates here in H-Unit. I'm sure that's because a lot of the inmates in my first class were mostly lifers, so nobody is leaving.

I think that is the reason most of the inmates in the North Block of the Q get along better than H-Unit. The macho thing is alive and well in prison but in H-Unit it's the way of an inmate's life, always looking over his shoulder and sleeping with one eye open the whole time.

I'm also glad some of these inmates in prison have outlets like music to blow off steam. If I can give some inmate a little peace of mind through the music class so he will not do something stupid either in prison or out in the streets, then I have done my job. That's all I can ask.

What a journey it must be to live in a prison. As the officer drops me off at the front post of H-Unit, he asks me if I can feel the vibe of the execution in the air tonight? I say, "No, why?" His answer to me is, "After every execution, there's a very tense mood that blankets the prison for about a week. There are no words that can explain it. You have a safe ride home." And with that said, the officer turns around and walks away not saying another word to me.

I sometimes feel very grateful to be teaching a prison music class even though it can be emotional for me, and a lot of the times, very dangerous. It's kind of like a Disneyland ride from Hell. I'm sure glad I can leave this mad house when music class is over at 9:00 p.m. It's an interesting place to visit or teach, but I wouldn't want to live there. Driving home I have to smile thinking that there is nothing like hearing inmates singing all together the words "Your cheatin' heart will tell on you" or "King of the Road." Maybe next week I will teach them the song "House of the Rising Sun."

May 18, 1999

I read in the newspaper this morning about a paroled inmate killing his ex-girlfriend and her new boyfriend. Seems he had been paroled out of San Quentin Prison only thirty days ago. He hunted her down and killed her over finding a new boyfriend; so he killed him too. He told the police that for the last two years of being locked up all he thought about was how to kill his ex-girlfriend and her new old man.

My day has been wild. I started out this morning at 9:00 a.m. singing for a special education preschool of three- to five-year-old kids. Then, from 10:30 a.m. till 2:00 p.m., I taught music class to kids at risk in low-income housing, lots of crime and gang bangers, but still kids. From 2:30 p.m. till 4:30 p.m., I worked with kids from two group homes. Now I am driving to San Quentin Prison, and tomorrow at 9:00 a.m., I will be teaching music back at Juvenile Hall.

It bothers me that kids have no time for their childhood any more. The pressures of life run high even as a kid. So when you add the fact of kids labeled "at risk," there is little chance of doing well in life. Some of the young kid gang bangers that I work with can't wait to go to prison. That is their dream in life, to spend some of their lives being locked up with other gang members; kicking it in San Quentin Prison.

As I drive through the east gate entrance I get that same creepy feeling in my body. There are always a lot of people from the outside waiting in line to be cleared, so they can go inside the prison. A lot of praying goes on in prison to help the time pass. I hear a couple of catcalls coming from the Ranch. It's still really strange for me to see inmates who look like ladies. And, in some cases even better, and sexier looking. One of them yells, "Hey Ringo, How's Paul doing these days" as he's giving me the thumbs up; or "Hey pretty boy, play me some ass-shaking music, Mr. Rock Star, or I'll kill ya." Then yells, "Only fucking with ya, just kidding, sorry."

After signing my name into the prison logbook and calling for my escort I'm greeted by my boss. She is here to tell me that I have been given twelve more weeks on my contract. She is not sure where I will be going to teach next; but she will know in the next couple of weeks. And I now have permission to bring in the guys in the band I play with on Saturday June 12th to perform for the inmates. We even get paid for it! I can't wait to see the looks on the faces of my fellow band mates. When my escort arrives, my boss says goodbye and good luck and that she will call me when she has the rest of the information.

My escort tonight is even more buffed out than the last couple of escorts. I'm shocked walking in, not one catcall from any inmates in H-Unit. Class is good. Seven inmates show up for music. The songs for the class are "Honky Tonk Women" and "Peaceful Easy Feeling." Music class runs very smooth tonight. Everyone sings and plays together. I think it's the first time for most of these students to sing and have some fun. It has been a hard road teaching music in H-Unit with a lot of hills to climb; but I'm getting there.

When I look into the eyes of some of the inmates here at the Q, I see a lot of little boys in men's bodies crying for a chance to be understood or just loved for who they really are. Every inmate has a story; a lot of broken dreams in prison.

About 8:30 p.m. one of my students stops playing his guitar and says "Buzzy, there's a couple of inmates in H-Unit that have a sex fetish for other inmates. They love the smell of a man's ass. I kid you not Buzzy! The scent drives these fuckin' sugar shorts nuts." All of the other inmates in class start laughing to the point of almost crying. I must have turned a pretty color of white because another inmate asks me, "Buzzy, are you going to throw up?" Before class is over, yet another inmate says to me, "You know all the stories you hear about inmates fucking other younger inmates, it's true. It's just to see the look on their faces. It's all true and sometimes it's even worse." Then he smiles and says, "Welcome to H-Unit my friend." Then it hits me, all of these inmates in H-Unit are testing me; seeing if they can get a reaction out of me; almost like the kids in Juvenile Hall. Always getting their kicks trying to gross me out and I'm not going for it. These inmates in class, for some reason, are trying to scare or intimidate me. I think it goes back to the code of prison life and the pecking order.

I don't say a word other than, "Let's play 'Old Time Rock n' Roll' one more time." As 9:00 p.m. rolls around once again two officers show up to unlock the office doors to let us out. Walking back across the main yard, I think about what the inmates in class had said about some old crusty con sucking on some young inmate's neck while jerking himself off. I sometimes hate this place because of what it does to some men. This place turns men into dogs, hunting for power, always looking to bite someone.

I feel numb. No feelings whatsoever. I have two more classes left on my contract in H-Unit. Then I hope that I can be moved back up the hill to North Block. Teaching a music class to the inmates is one thing, but these inmates in H-Unit love to fuck with my mind.

I hope the last two classes run smoothly. It would feel good knowing that I left the inmates in H-Unit on a good note. I can't wait to see the looks on all of the kids' faces in Juvenile Hall tomorrow morning when I share some of my stories of San Quentin Prison with them. Some of the kids will never believe me. They will have to check out this place for themselves. That's the sad part.

May 25, 1999

Tonight is my last class at H-Unit. I've been given another twelve-week contract to North Block in twenty days. So tonight I'll recap everything that I've taught my students in the last twelve weeks of the music program.

Teaching music in H-Unit is something that I'll never forget. There were a couple of nights that I would sit in my truck after class and cry, or throw up because I was so freaked out.

This morning I threw out all of my denim shirts and blue jeans because when I put them on I looked and felt like an inmate. How fucked up is that? San Quentin Prison gets under your skin, sometimes without your knowing it and then it's too late. The damage is done. It's odd how many different impressions people outside of the walls have of prison life.

I have to stop off at the local music store before coming to the Q to pick up strings and picks for a kind of going-away gift for my H-Unit class. Picks in prison are like gold to the inmate musicians. Guitar strings are even more valuable because when an inmate breaks a string, he either has to wait for me to bring in a set of new strings or tie the old string together and hope for the best.

Before I leave the music store, I hear a couple of stupid jokes and I'm asked some really dumb questions by the guys behind the counter. Things like, "Hey Buzzy, how's the food in Quentin," or "Don't drop your guitar Buzzy because you'll have to bend over to pick it up." Working or teaching in a prison changes your way of thinking.

As I drive into the east gate prison entrance I can smell the bay and see a flock of seagulls flying over the Q. The cool wind blowing on my face feels good. The sounds of doors slamming or alarms going off, inmates always talking, officers' keys swinging back and forth, all of this going on all the time makes for a lot of noise. I've been told that's why most of the inmates are so cranky, because no one gets a lot of sleep in prison. In the winter, the cells are always cold and damp. And in the summer, the cells and rooms inside of the prison can reach up to 110°.

I heard a story about a teacher who had passed out because it had gotten so hot in the classroom. When I sign in tonight the officer on duty at H-Unit tells me some of the inmates have been waiting for me for about an hour already. There must be five or six hundred inmates walking around the main yard. Some are playing basketball, while some are doing push-ups. Some inmates are playing checkers, while others are just doing nothing, and then, some inmates try hard to do everything they can to keep out of trouble.

Most of the inmates I've been in contact with look like bikers, or scary crank dealers. Most of my students have lots of prison tattoos. Some have shaved heads and no teeth. But other inmates in class look like fourth grade schoolteachers, very preppy. And then, there are inmates who just love being locked up and told what to do. Those are the kind that creep me out. In a lot of ways, tonight's class is very sad and in other ways extremely moving to see how much these inmates have learned about music and themselves.

After roll call is over, I give each student about five picks apiece and then change a couple of strings on one of the inmate's guitars that really need changing. One of my students raises his hand and asks me if I can teach the class the song "Jailhouse Rock" or

"Folsom Prison Blues." For a moment I'm not sure if this inmate is joking with me or not. Then another inmate smiles and says that he would not mind singing either song because he knows all of the words to both the songs. So, for the first hour of class I teach the class both songs while a couple of inmates sing the words. I have to laugh out loud when one of the inmates shouts out, "I want to kill somebody because I can't sing and play these songs at the same time." I can tell by how much fun everyone is having that it has been a long time since these inmates have let their guards down. As class comes to an end, one by one the inmates in class tell me that I have done a great job teaching them music. They also tell me that I am very respected around the prison because I come to the Q. "You've got big balls my friend," one of the inmates tells me. Right before 9:00 p.m., another inmate says to me, "The other inmates in this music class are somewhat shy about telling you how much the class and you coming into this fucked up hell hole, week after week really means to them. So here's a little going away and thank you card from me and all of the other inmates at H-Unit." My students have grown as musicians and as men too. To be able to work as a team is a great thing for everyone in class.

When I open up the envelope, I see the card is from the Marin Collection, printed exclusively for the Marin Independent Journal newspaper. How it ended up in the Q, God only knows. The picture on the front of the card has a color photo of the Golden Gate Bridge and the Marin Headlands. I am guessing that it was taken from an airplane. When I open up the card, it reads, "Thanks for music time, your time and the time you spent with us to make us just a mo 'little happen-en!'"; it's signed by all of the inmates in music class.

After twelve weeks of playing with my mind, class after class, these inmates finally show me that they do have a lot of feelings for me. They just couldn't show it before because that means weakness to the other inmates. After class has ended, one inmate who hardly said one word to me the whole twelve weeks takes my hand and with a tear in his eye says to me, "Thank you for caring about old cons like me. God bless you Buzzy; have a safe ride home."

Then he smiles and puts his hand on my shoulder. Another inmate says "Okay, Alice, knock it off; here comes the dickheads to make us go to bed," as yet another inmate says, "You're going to make all of us start crying, you shit heads, stop all of the love shit. You're giving me a hard on."

The good-byes move me. The feeling of loss is running high tonight because this is the last class. Looking back at the last eight months that I've been teaching the prison music program, I feel that I have grown one thousand percent as a musician and as a person. It has given me a new meaning to the word freedom. I never set out to be a role model, teacher, or mentor, just a good person who plays music and believes in being honest and having dreams for the future.

As the officer unlocks the door to let us out, one of the inmates looks over towards me and winks, then smiles saying, "Take care of yourself, boss. Have a drink for me sometime and thanks again."

The Band Performs in Prison

This is the day that I've been waiting for. Today I'm bringing in the band of musicians I play with. We are going to play a little concert for the inmates at San Quentin Prison. It's now 8:00 a.m., Saturday morning. We have to be at the east gate entrance before 9:30 a.m. in order to be checked in by the officers on duty. Every one of us has to pass gate clearance; otherwise we can't go in and play music.

This morning is very foggy, so we will have to drive a little slower. There are three vans full of musicians following each other down to the prison so none of us will get lost. One van has the guitars with my good friend and band roadie, Daddy G, and me driving. There is another van with the other guitar player, Stevie, Rick the drummer, and our other band roadie, Brent, driving. The last van is carrying Kent, the bass player, and Steve, our sax player. When Daddy G and I arrived at the band's meeting place, we were both shocked to see all four of my fellow band mates dressed up in black pants, white shirts and black vests. They looked like a bunch of penguins. I had called everyone the night before to tell them what not to wear along with the dos and don'ts of being in a prison with a bunch of inmates.

I thought I had made it really clear to everyone. I don't think my fellow band mates get the full picture of prison yet, but by the time this day is over, every one of us will have a story to tell. Playing as a band for the inmates, instead of by myself is going to be a big rush for me and a bigger rush for my former inmate students who have never seen me play and sing with a band. I can't wait to see the looks on the faces of my fellow band mates when we are greeted by the inmates and staff. Even after my phone calls last night to each member, I could tell they did not have a clue about what to expect.

The main rules I tell them are these: first, if asked by an inmate, "Where do you guys live," make up a name of a town. Don't tell anyone in prison where you really live. Don't give out any information about your family or yourself to anybody. Secondly, do not wander off with any inmates. In other words, do not get too friendly with any inmates. Stay with each other as a group. And the three most important rules to remember while in a prison are, don't run, keep a picture ID on yourself at all times, and don't stare at the inmates. My boss warned me that there would be about one thousand to twelve hundred inmates today in the main prison yard at one time watching the band play. With this many inmates together at one time, chances are good there can be some trouble.

I have this feeling that the guys in the band are thinking it's just another gig to them, no big deal. But that is about to change. The goofy look on their faces will go away as soon as they enter the prison and sign their names in the logbook. Four band members looking like penguins. Thank God, Daddy G, Brent, and myself are all wearing green, black and gray clothes. The inmates will look at my fellow band members like, "What the fuck are these guys all dressed up for. It's a prison for God's sake." The band members look like a Holiday Inn band. It's just asking for trouble. I wish them luck, because in prison everyone is on their own. The officers on duty will, hopefully, look out for us. Besides, my boss told me that I'm very respected in prison now because everyone loves music, and I'm willing to teach it here. I'm what is called a Free Man — someone from the outside who brings a gift to the inmates that changes their life.

When we pull up to the east gate entrance of the prison, Daddy G says to me, "Strange looking place, Buzzy. When do we leave?" Then he says, "People can't pay to see this shit. This place is crazy. I want to go home." I look over at him and say, "Daddy G, this feeling that you are having right now is nothing! Wait until you

get behind the walls and smell the air. You haven't seen anything yet."
I can see by the looks on the guys' faces that they are starting to
think about what lies ahead. No one is saying a word.

As soon as everyone has signed their names in the logbook and
we are cleared to go inside, we park the vans in the prison public
parking lot, except one, Daddy G's van. Since I have a green card, I'm
cleared to drive around some parts of the prison. So from this point,
I drive. Everyone piles into the van and for fifteen minutes, I give them
a mini-tour of San Quentin Prison.

First I take them past H-Unit, then the Ranch. I show them
as much as I can in the time we have. Not one word is spoken.
Not one. I can tell everyone is stunned. This place leaves everyone
speechless. Once the little tour is over and I have parked the van,
I ask, "Is everyone okay?" Again, no one says a word. They just nod
their heads. With a smile, I say, "Let's go gentlemen. Let's go have
some real fun!"

There are thirty steps that everyone has to climb in order
to get from the prison parking lot to the next prison checkpoint.
We are greeted at the top of the stairs by two officers. The first
thing we are told is open up our guitar cases and the sax case, too.
I set down my case along with Stevie, Kent, and our sax player, Steve.
As we are opening our cases, to our surprise one of the officers starts
yelling out, "What's in that pill container? Open it! Open it right
now." I can't believe this officer is flipping out over this pill bottle
in Stevie's guitar case. Stevie glances over towards me with a face
as white as a ghost. I say, "Better open it up, Stevie. What's in it?"
He tells me, "I don't know. I forgot I had it in my case. Who knows."
While the officer leans over Stevie's back waiting for him to open up
the bottle, the guys in the band hold their breath wondering what
is going to happen next. All I can think is, "Great. We are all in trouble
now." At this point, Stevie picks up the pill container, twists off
the cap, looks inside, smiles at all of us and says, "Thank God, it's just
screws and nuts for my guitar. No big deal."

After the officers check out the rest of the cases we all move on to the next checkpoint. At the last checkpoint, everyone is still speechless. No one is saying a word. Rick, the drummer, whispers to me, "Buzzy, this place gives me the creeps. I can't believe you come in here to teach every week. Are you sure we're going to be safe?" The officer who is the band's escort smiles and says, "Boys, you've got nothing to worry about. Because these inmates that you're going to meet are ready to hear some rock and roll." The other officer says, "I can tell you guys are a bit nervous and a little awe struck; but it's really going to be okay. No one's going to fuck with you while you're here. Just mind your mouths and everything should go fine."

We walk along an old paved road leading down to the main prison yard. When we turn the last corner of the oldest part of the prison, we are greeted by about one thousand buffed out inmates, either walking around or just hanging out. Except for the two officers escorting us, there are no other officers in sight. As far as we can see, a sea of blue denim. We are truly about to be on our own in a matter of minutes.

As we walk down the hill, I'm welcomed by many of my past students. I'm given lots of high fives and some hugs, too. For a moment it feels like a high school class reunion. My boss arrives with a big smile on her face. She shakes all the guys' hands, thanking them for coming into the prison to play music for the inmates. She tells me again that I have built up a lot of trust among the inmates. "Buzzy, if the inmates trust you, then they'll trust the guys in the band with you." By now, more and more inmates are crowding around the band asking questions like, "What kinds of music do you play and how long have you guys been playing music with each other?"

About this time, Stevie the guitar player, leans over towards me and asks, "Buzzy, where are the bathrooms? I have to pee real bad and I can't hold it until we're done with our set. Just ask one of your students where the can is, will you please?" So without thinking, I turn around and ask one of the inmates who had been a student of mine. "Hey, where's the bathrooms? My buddy, Stevie, has to pee pretty bad and we've got to start our set in about twenty minutes." The inmates around us that hear our conversation stop talking and begin looking at both Stevie and me. After a few moments, one of the inmates finally points towards an old red brick building and says, "See that brick wall there? That's the mens' bathroom. No shyness here, no one has privacy in prison. So, if you have to piss, there's your bathroom, boss."

I look over at Stevie, "Well, there you go, my friend. You are on your own. If you are going to go pee, I'd hurry up because time is ticking."

I can see by the look on Stevie's face, he is not sure if these inmates are telling him the truth or not. But after a few minutes of mulling it over, he turns and heads for the red brick wall. As he gets closer, he stops, turns his head slowly looking back at all of us, and, of course, we all wave at him.

One of the inmates standing with us shouts, "Good luck." Another inmate says, "If you want me to help you, I'll be right there to hold it." After ten minutes of looking back at all of us waving at him and giving him the thumbs up, Stevie at last pees! When he walks back to join us, some of the inmates slap Stevie on his back and give him high fives for peeing on the prison wall. I guess it's a big deal for a musician to pee on the prison wall. Stevie doesn't say one word or smile. I think he's in shock.

Before the band does our set, other prison bands perform. Two blues bands and one blues funk band, all inmates. The inmates are running the PA, too. All of the amps, drums, and keyboards, everything is owned by the prison. So at this point, except for my boss and a couple of officers, the guys in the band and I are the only people from the outside. Our escort officers tells us to have a good time and that they too are leaving, but will be back in about an hour or so, leaving us all alone with about one thousand inmates milling around.

By the time it becomes our turn to play our set, we are pumped up. The first song is "Great Balls of Fire," then "Old Time Rock and Roll," followed by "Rock This Town." Fifteen fast songs, and one slow song, "My Girl," by the Temptations. One hour of great party music. The inmates come alive. They are all dancing, swaying, and singing to the music. It is something to see. You can feel the vibe of happiness all around. As we play, all the musician inmates are giving us the thumbs up, while checking out our guitars. We end our set with "Sharp Dressed Man," a ZZ Top song. Everyone is having a great time. The inmates are chanting the words, "Every girl crazy 'bout a sharp dressed man," and dancing with each other, as their fists are raised above their heads. I wish I could take a group picture. The penitentiary is definitely rockin'. It's weird seeing some of the inmates holding hands or kissing while we are playing the song "My Girl." Nothing is crazier than seeing a couple of mean-looking inmates with shaved heads and lots of tattoos sucking on each other's necks. Wow!

As I turn off the amp and put away my guitar, one of the inmates that played before us walks up to me and asks me, "I was wondering if you have any phone numbers of any booking agents? Because I'm getting out of here in two years. Is it possible I can get your phone number and address? I'll look you up when I get out." All I can say to him is, "Sorry, my friend, I can't help you. But good luck." And with that, I shake his hand.

We start walking back up the hill to leave, stop and look back down at the inmates. What a sight seeing inmates that look like women, but with lots of tattoos walking around trolling for fresh fish (young boys). I say, "Okay guys, it's time to leave. Let's go." Walking back to the van nobody says a word. Rick is white as a ghost. Brent feels sick and Daddy G just wants to go home to throw up. Everyone seems glad to be going home. We are met at the top of the driveway by the same two officers who had escorted us into the prison. And here they are to bring us back out. The one officer looks at Rick and Brent and says, "Boys, you don't look very good. Are ya all going to be all right?" Kent, the bass player, says, "I can tell you that I feel like shit." And Rick adds, "Yeah, my head's killing me. I need a drink."

Stevie looks at me and grins, not saying a word. So I say, "What's up big guy? What's on your mind?" He smiles and says, "Let's do it again sometime. I had a blast."

I'm glad everything went smoothly today. It feels like the making of the Blues Brothers movie. Today is something the band, will never forget. As we are being checked back out, one of the escorting officers tells us the first inmate band members are all lifers. He says, "Boys, those inmates that played before you guys will die in here. Now it's a damn shame because some of those assholes can sing and play pretty good. How about you boys, did you enjoy yourselves in prison today?" No one answers him.

We walk back to the vans and it seems like days have gone by. We are all shell-shocked. It had to be the wildest ride that any of us has ever taken. Brent, our six-foot, seven-inch, two hundred-and-eighty-pound roadie, asks me, "Buzzy, I didn't think women can come inside San Quentin Prison and hang out with the inmates. I saw about five chicks dressed up in denim looking pretty damn sexy. There was a black lady that smiled at me and then licked her lips. I can't believe that the prison lets this kind of thing go on. What's up with that?"

I tell him, "Well, Brent, I hate to be the one to break the bad news to ya, but those chicks that were hitting on you are guy inmates. That's what's up with that, my good friend."

Driving home, my friend Daddy G keeps saying, "Holy shit, Buzzy. That was out there. Way out there! That place is out of control. Let's go have a beer." I tell him, "Daddy G, when we get back to my house, let's have two beers each!"

Back in North Block

July 13, 1999

I'm starting my new music class tonight. I'm going back to the North Block right next to Death Row. I have been inside San Quentin Prison thirty-two times and it still freaks me out, no getting around it. The Q is a city that runs on its own terms. This blue denim city has gangs, junkies, drug running by inmates' families to make money, and some inmates with AIDS or Hepatitis C, taking orders from the top dog inmates of each race. They call all of the shots in this city behind closed walls.

I have been away from the prison for about three weeks. The last time I was here, it was with the band I play with and boy was that wild. I don't miss H-Unit at all. I hope that I am never asked to go back.

Walking into the North Block of the prison feels a lot better than walking into H-Unit. The stress vibe is less here. My boss tells me I have between ten and twelve new inmates signed up for music class.

I'm told by one of the officers on duty that those big old factories in San Quentin that face Highway 101 are where the inmates make everything from box springs to tables and chairs, anything to make money for the prison. It costs a lot of money to run this penitentiary. The inmates have jobs to help build things, so the prison can make money towards paying some of the bills. Inmates who have jobs get paid $2.00 a day. The main cell block is five stories tall, with one hundred cells in a row, double back to back with two inmates per cell. There are yellow lines painted everywhere. No inmates can walk past these yellow lines, ever. I'm also amazed at how clean everything is in this part of the prison;

79

even the floors look pretty clean. I sometimes wonder how long I will keep coming here. It's almost like a drug. I sometimes want to be taken deeper inside the prison, go to the heart of the Q. I have been told by a few staff that if I ever want a tour, all I have to do is ask one of the officers on duty.

As I get closer to the Education Room, I have to pass the Max Shack. I look inside the office window and see two lady officers talking. I open up the door to say hello and one of the lady officers says to me, "Who are you and what do you want"? I tell her I'm the guitar teacher for the inmates and that I'm going to be here every Tuesday night for twelve weeks. After a phone call to Control, I'm given a panic button for protection. She says, "If there's any trouble in the room, just push that little red button and all hell will break loose. Welcome to San Quentin Prison."

As I'm opening up the door to the Education Room, an inmate walks up to me and asks if he can join the guitar music class. He tells me, "Boss, I only have four years and two months left to do here in the pen. So learning how to play the guitar would make my time go by a little easier." I tell him I have nothing to do with that part of the class. He would have to ask someone from the prison staff. I add, "My boss has the last word on this music program, not me. I just teach the class, sorry."

While we are talking, six inmates show up for class. Everyone needs new strings. Thank God I have ten sets of new strings and lots of picks. So after ninety minutes of restringing every inmate's guitar, we are ready to get down and learn some songs. I teach the class "Johnny B. Good," "Old Time Rock n' Roll," and "Gloria." There is only one inmate who can't play the guitar; but boy can he sing. He sings his ass off. He can sing like Chuck Berry; but he looks like Charlie Manson. So I let him sing all three songs. When we end the class everyone thanks me for coming in and teaching them music. The inmate who sang all night shakes my hand and says, "Thanks for letting me sing, boss. You're okay. This class is going to be a lot of fun. You got nothing to worry about while teaching us, because we're going to watch your back. See ya next week. Have a safe ride home."

These inmates are nothing like the inmates in H-Unit. While they are playing "Gloria," some close their eyes and rock back and forth while keeping the beat with their feet. This is going to be a great twelve-week music class.

As I close the door of the Education Room, I decide to say goodbye to the lady officers, since I had to return the panic button to the Max Shack. The door to the Max Shack is open, so I pop my head inside to say good night; one of the lady officers asks me. "I've heard from a couple of the other officers that you would like to take a little tour of Camp Quentin. Is that true?" So, I say, "It is true. I wouldn't mind seeing some of the prison sometime." She smiles, "Honey, this is your lucky night. I'll take you on a little ride right now. Leave your guitar with my partner in the Shack and follow me." First stop, the prison dining hall. I ask her how long she has been working in the Q and she tells me just over three years.

When she opens up the door to the dining hall, all the inmates stop eating and talking and turn their heads our way. No one says a word. Everyone just looks at us like we're aliens. And we are, aliens from the land of freedom. I feel a cold chill as this big steel door closes behind us. One by one the inmates begin talking to each other again. For just a moment I feel like the one who is all alone in the prison. I'm the different one, because of my clothes. I have no denim or uniform on. I wear street clothes and that opens up the inmates' eyes pretty quickly because they wonder who I am. Thank God, in my case, a couple of the inmates who are eating dinner had been in one of my first music classes. They walk up to me, shake my hand, ask how I've been doing lately, and how the music class is going. It makes the moment go by a little easier for me.

Besides the inmates, the first thing I notice in the dining hall are these huge murals on the walls. The murals, twelve feet tall and nearly one hundred feet long cover California history from frontier days to the frenzy of the World War II homefront. Executed in reddish-brown oil, the works are a panorama of popular images from movie stars to field hands set against an iconic background of agriculture and history. There are a couple of optical tricks: a cable car standing at a turnaround appears to move as you walk by, as does a plane being hammered together by defense workers. The officer tells me that one inmate started painting the murals around 1953 at the request of prison officials who were looking to decorate some new walls put up when the old dining hall was divided into sections. She says, "As the story's been told to me that inmate worked on the murals for two years, standing on scaffolding that was pushed around by a couple of other inmates."

As we leave the prison dining hall, I get a few inmates blowing me kisses and winking at me. Then the officer asks me if I would like to see some of the inmates' cells. "Sure," I say, "Are you sure it's okay for me to do that?"

"No problem," she says. "You'll get a kick out of this freak show. Follow me."

We walk into one of the cellblocks and boy does it stink. There is no fresh air in the cells, plus everyone is farting. The cells are the size of a small bathroom, with two inmates to each cell, plus the toilet. Too tight a space for me!

There are TV sets in some of the cells and in other cells, a couple of inmates are either writing letters or reading books. As the officer and I walk past the cells, I can hear a couple of catcalls coming from a few of the inmates. As we get deeper inside the cellblock the smell gets stronger, almost to the point where I start to get sick. I think the lady officer senses that I'm not feeling all that good, because she turns to me and says, "Look, the air is getting pretty thick inside here. I'd say it's time to leave. Is that okay with you?"

I reply, "If we have to go because of the smell, I'm okay to leave."

So within five minutes, we are walking back out of the cellblock unit. I tell her, "Thanks for taking me on a little tour of the Q. I'll see you next Tuesday; and thanks again for taking your time to show me around." Driving home, I thank God a thousand times for blessing me with the gift of music and for letting me smell fresh air again.

July 27, 1999

Last night before falling asleep I found myself channel surfing with the TV set and I came across the MTV show called "Scared Straight." It's a show where cameras are brought into a prison somewhere in the United States and they film bad ass inmates yelling at young tough boys trying to make these kids cry, trying to break them down. Some of these boys are labeled high risk or young gang bangers that are already in a lot of trouble with the law. So their probation officer has them sent down to prison to see if this is the kind of life that they really want to live.

Some of the inmates were telling these kids that they would be someone's bitch in prison within seventy-two hours after arriving. Other inmates were spitting at a couple of the kids. They said to one young white boy, "Bitch, I can trade you for a pack of gum and not really give a flying fuck about you. Predator or prey, what do you think about that, bitch?" One kid cried and another kid threw up.

After about forty-five minutes of watching this show, I had to turn it off. It scared the shit out of me and I work inside of a penitentiary. I will never watch that show again. Why a kid would ever want to live his life in a prison is way beyond my understanding.

As I come upon the east gate entrance, the sun is just going down. It's casting a shadow on the prison walls that makes the prison look even creepier. Once I park my truck and I'm cleared to go inside, I walk over to the 4 Post to get the inmates' movement sheet. But the officer tells me, "Sorry, son, there's no movement sheet for your music class tonight. There's no way you can get to class without the movement sheet. So why don't you just wait right here and I'll be right with you."

The very next moment buzzers start blowing away, blue lights start flashing from side to side, and horns are blowing so loud, it hurts my ears. I try to ask the officer, "What the hell's going on?" But by now the officer behind the desk starts barking out orders like, "Unlock the guns, call for more back up."

While all hell's breaking loose, I look over to my left side and see these three inmates sitting cross-legged on the floor, just outside of the office. One of the inmates grins at me and says, "You might as well come on over here and sit down, because you're not going anywhere for awhile. Plus, they're not going to let you out of here just yet. It's going to take a little while to settle this place down." The inmate sitting next to him says, "You're the Guitar Man that I've been hearing about. We can talk about music until the bells and lights are turned off."

Officers are now running past me; the sound of keys hitting their belts as they yell things about lock downs, fighting inmates, and getting out their guns is pretty staggering. After what seems like hours of sitting on the floor, everything just stops — the lights, horns, officers yelling, everything, like it began, without warning.

As I walk back over to the 4 Post, the officer tells me to just go home. There will be no class tonight. I ask him if I can get the inside phone number to the prison so that I can call next time before I drive all the way here. After giving me the prison inside line, I'm told to go home and try again next week.

Once I have signed the book and drive out the east gate entrance, I have to wait in traffic on the Bay Bridge for another forty-five minutes. Driving home I think about being trapped in the middle of a lock down at San Quentin Prison and how bad I felt for those few minutes wondering what was going to happen next. I will call next week and save myself the heartbreak.

August 3, 1999

It has been really hot in northern California for the last four days. Today the temperature is up to 105°, so it's hot and sticky inside my truck driving to the Q.

After getting cleared by the east gate officer on duty, I drive in and park my truck. It's hard for me to breathe because the air is so hot and very heavy. The sweat is running down my face by the time I reach the classroom door. When I open the door, the heat in the room is unbearable. It must be ten degrees hotter in the room than outside. While I air out the room, I wait outside for about a half an hour watching the prison come alive after dinnertime.

There are hundreds of inmates walking from the prison dining hall. An endless stream of blue denim coming and going. While I'm standing next to the classroom door, two male officers walk up to me really slowly. Both officers are really big, one black, the other white. I begin to wonder what is up with these guys. As they get a little closer, the white officer asks me in a low voice, "Hey slick, do you know where I can buy a good low-priced guitar?" The other officer asks me, "I've been wanting to take up music for awhile now. Is it very hard to learn how to play the guitar? I just want to learn how to play music, so I can relax, that's all!"

So for the next ten minutes I explain the best prices for guitars and some of the music stores in the Bay Area where they can buy one. While I'm telling these officers where to buy a guitar I hear the sound of an ambulance coming. The horns and lights are going off and all the inmates move, parting the way so the prison ambulance can come through. One of the officers that I'm talking with says, "Some bonehead must have gotten hurt in a fight or been jumped by another inmate. That's life in a prison. It happens all the time. It's no big deal, everyday life in the Q."

As my students start to arrive for class, the two officers and I say our good-byes. Once inside the room, I begin to sweat. As I wipe my face with a towel, I say, "Man, is it hot tonight or what?" This older black inmate smiles at me and says, "Shit, boss, this ain't nothing. You ought to sleep in one of our cells for a couple of nights. The heat can get unbearable sometimes. It's just starting to get warm. Wait until it's 110°, that's when the parties start. Nothing like cooking a bunch of old cons. It makes all of us a little jumpy when it gets really hot."

I will keep my mouth shut next time. After roll call is over, I teach my class the songs "My Girl" and "Stand By Me." I find the class to be very mellow tonight. I am sure the heat helps a lot.

The smell of underarm is strong in class. At one point, I think I'm going to gag. But, class goes very smoothly, except that the room is a lot hotter than outside.

August 10, 1999

The heat has not let up for the last ten days. It has been in the low 100s. Tonight I'm told the music class is being moved to another building for a couple of weeks. The building that we will be using for music class is in one of the older parts of the prison; it's called Room C. I have to walk down three flights of stairs. At the end of the stairwell, there are three classrooms and two bathrooms, one for the inmates and one for staff and the teachers. The bathroom for the staff has a door on it, but the inmates' bathroom has no door. It's all open. Anyone can look at one of the inmates going to the bathroom at any time. The officer tells me it will be about ten minutes before any inmates will show up for music class.

By the time that I get to the room I am going to use for music class, my shirt is soaked. I have dry mouth and I have to pee really badly. I go right to the staff bathroom, pee, wash my hands and face, and then get a little drink of water. All before any of my students show up for class. Room C smells old and musty. I open up the room so that it can air out a little. One by one inmates start walking in. I have nine students tonight. I notice on the inmate movement sheet that there are two new students in class.

As the last inmate enters the room, he looks at me, smiles and asks, "Is your first name Buzzy? Are you the guy that I've been reading about and that I've seen on TV"? He goes on to say, "You work with a lot of kids at risk, don't you? I've heard about you for a while. You're always in the news. And just think, I'm now meeting you here in the Q; shit." All I can say is, "Yep that's me." A cold chill runs up and down my back. I'm left speechless. To have inmates know things about me or my family does not make me feel real comfortable. Inmates can and do use information about what they know to intimidate staff or officers. I have always wanted to be a famous rock n' roll musician but not to inmates in prison.

Three inmates do not have guitars. So they and I walk over to the Arts Building where the prison guitars are kept.

After picking out three guitars for the inmates, I close and lock up the room and then start walking back to Room C. We could not have walked more than one hundred feet when out of nowhere I start hearing someone yelling out the word "escort." Every inmate in sight stops talking and walks up to the first wall in sight and puts his nose on the wall, not moving, not saying a single word — noses touching the wall, like programmed zombies. With every moment, the word "escort" grows louder. By now my heart is crawling out of my chest, beating faster with every yell of the word "escort."

So here I am, standing all by myself looking around at all these inmates with their faces pushed up against the prison wall and then I see what the inmates in San Quentin cannot and do not see. Four big officers escorting this little black inmate dressed in a blue jump suit into the prison. This little black inmate has handcuffs and leg cuffs on; and as they pass by me, he looks at me and smiles, looking almost proud.

As the officers walk him by me, no one says a word. Time stands still for me as I stand there, stunned by what I am seeing. The word "escort" fades in the air. One by one, inmates start pushing themselves away from the prison wall. All their noses and foreheads have the imprint of the wall on them. I think, "What the hell just happened?" I have never seen anything like that in my life. As we start walking back to Room C, I get up enough guts to ask one of my inmate students what had happened. He explains to me that blue jump suits are for first-time inmates coming into the prison. For the protection of first-timers, inmates are not allowed to see their faces while being brought in. That way, poof, an inmate just shows up in the middle of this little city called San Quentin Prison. He tells me, "It's a lot safer for the new inmates that are young. This way it takes a little longer to get fucked up in prison. Otherwise these fish would be hit on in hours, instead of days."

Once we arrive back at the room we play and sing our hearts out. The songs are "On the Road Again," "I Feel Good" and "Evil Ways." Thank God, the rest of the night goes smoothly. Very easy sailing, except for me thinking of that big black officer yelling "escort" at the top of his lungs. What a way to live one's life.

After class is over, I stop by to drop off some paperwork at the front officer's desk. I talk to the night officer about my class and how stunned I was about the officers yelling "escort" while bringing in some young inmate. He tells me, "Son, you should have been here last Saturday. There was a prison riot going on that almost kicked our ass. We had about eighty inmates fighting with each other. What a mess. We had to call for two alarms." He goes on to tell me that he has worked in San Quentin for twenty years and he can only remember three times that the prison has had to use the two-alarm warning. He grins and says in a low voice, "It's got to be pretty fucked up to call for two-alarms; but when the dogs start showing their teeth, you've got to put them in their place right away."

This place has such a long history of heartbreak and pain. There is shit that goes on in here between inmates that still blows my mind. After we say our good-byes I walk out of the prison and sit by the bay watching the cars drive over the Bay Bridge, smelling the fresh cool air of summer. Driving home, I wonder what happens when the prison calls for a two-alarm. I almost asked the officer, but deep down I don't think I really wanted to know.

August 17, 1999

I was reminded today that Elvis Presley died twenty-two years ago. The radio's been blasting out Elvis songs all day. So I thought I would show the inmates the songs "Jailhouse Rock," "Little Sister," and "Ready Teddy."

As I pull into the prison staff parking lot, a news bulletin comes on the radio cutting off "Burning Love." The DJ says that the Bay Area has just had an earthquake registering 5.0. The country of Turkey was hit yesterday and a number of people have died in that one. As I sign my name into the logbook, I ask the officer on duty if he had felt anything shake. He tells me some of the prison staff and a lot of the inmates had felt some shaking, but that he had not felt anything where he was standing. As I walk around inside of San Quentin I keep thinking that I still have to walk down three flights of stairs below ground to get to Room C for music class. While I wait for my students to arrive, I hope that there will not be any aftershocks. The thought of being trapped inside San Quentin Prison is terrifying.

I end up with eight inmates. One inmate asks me if he can play and sing this song he wrote about being locked up in a prison. I tell him, "I would love to hear your song, my friend." At this point all the inmates sit down and let their fellow inmate sing and play his heart out. I must say, he rocks out. It's a really good song. After he's done, I shake his hand and tell him, "Great job. It sounds really good. Don't ever stop writing music. Maybe some day you can record your songs." He looks at me kind of sad and says, "Boss, I'm a lifer. There's no way that I'm ever getting out of here, unless I break out or die. But thanks for the nice words bro. Maybe you can bring in a tape recorder. Is that possible"? I'm sorry to tell him it's impossible to bring anything into the prison, let alone a tape recorder. There is no way the officers would ever let me. The rest of the night the class runs very smoothly except for me worrying the whole time whether the old building would ever fall down because of an aftershock. Of course the inmates could have cared less about anything other than singing and playing Elvis songs.

Before class ends, one of the inmates says with a grin, "Fuck the earthquake, fuck this prison, and fuck Elvis, too. He's dead anyhow. But other than that, I love all of you fucks." And then in a great Elvis voice he says, "I've got to go now. God bless you and thank you very much." We all laugh as we put away our guitars. Sometimes I can forget I'm teaching lifers in a prison.

August 31, 1999

It has been two weeks since I have been in San Quentin. Last Tuesday every inmate was put on lock down because there were tools missing from the prison shop class. I read in the newspaper that a couple of claw hammers and three screwdrivers were taken. That is not the kind of stuff the prison staff wants floating around. But they found everything a couple of days later. It turned up in the main yard. Boy, could the inmates have a party with those kind of tools.

As I check into the prison tonight, I can see the officers are all on their toes making sure the prison is safe. An officer who is going home tells me there had been a gang fight about four hours ago, so feelings are running very high among the officers. Right now there is zero tolerance for the inmates. The Mexicans have been fighting with the black inmates over control rights in the prison.

Even locked up, inmates cannot get along with each other. What is wrong with this picture? There is a building in the courtyard that faces the prison church. The staff calls it the Adjustment Center. The inmates housed in this unit are put in there because they cannot get along with the other inmates. They are way too mean and violent to handle. The philosophy is that inmates housed in this building have to be ridden and broken hard, like breaking in a wild horse and sooner or later, they will come around. Sadly, they all do. It's just a matter of time.

After getting the inmate movement sheet, I walk down the stairs to Room C and wait for my students to show up. By 6:30 p.m., all I have are three white guys. Everyone of color is on lock down. I notice all three of these inmates have teeth missing. Their heads are shaved and they have tattoos everywhere, including their head and neck. Two of the inmates look really mean. Their fingers are stained a brownish yellow from smoking cigarettes.

The songs tonight are "My Girl," "Jumpin' Jack Flash" and "Feelin' All Right." One song for every inmate. The students sit in their chairs trying as hard as they can to learn these songs. For a moment they become almost childlike. Very open to learning music now that they are locked up for life. One of the inmates keeps looking out the window of Room C, laughing to himself and saying things like, "There he goes; he's trolling; he's dropping the line; bang! He's got the fish!" By now I have stopped playing the guitar. I stand up and walk over to the window wondering what I am going to see and there in the main prison yard are two old cons kissing on a young inmate in a corner. Both inmates are touching this young Mexican inmate, both laughing at their new catch. I can tell by the look on this inmate's face that the dignity of his youth is all but gone and the rest is about to leave him by tonight. I cannot watch anymore. I want to throw up, again. I want to go home. By now the other two inmates in class start feeling sorry for me because one of them asks me, "Buzzy, you're looking a little white in the face. Are you going to be okay?" As the other inmate walks away from the window, he looks at me, saying, "Just to let you know, fish have three choices in prison. One: Having sex with other inmates. Two: Joining a gang by killing another inmate. But remember if you kill someone in prison, you're never going to see freedom ever again. And three: You can kill yourself. Most of the inmates that are first timers just go for the sex. That's the life of a fish. It makes life in prison a little easier if you don't piss off anybody while staying in San Quentin."

After class is over, I just put my guitar away, saying very little. What can I say? I'm at a loss for words. Driving home, I keep thinking of that young inmate's face. It is something I will never forget. It made my heart hurt seeing his face while those two old cons were kissing on him. I'm going to share this story with the "tough boyz" in Juvenile Hall.

October 5, 1999

One of the hardest things for me to do while teaching music in San Quentin Prison is to think about everything that I am going to say before I say it, and to remember never to make jokes about the prison or to ever tell a joke to any inmate. Also, never ask too many questions. And the biggest rule for me is never to say "what" to any inmates. The word "what" can get me in a lot of trouble. It opens up a big can of worms that I would like to keep closed. If you ask an inmate a question, you might not want to hear the answer.

I have missed the last five weeks, due to a lot of lock downs in the prison. I got the word from my boss yesterday that I would be going back to the H-Unit for my next music class. I am not real thrilled about going back to the crazy farm; but I will try it one more time. It couldn't be any worse than the last time.

As I pull up to the east gate entrance, I'm told by one of the officers on night duty to pull my truck over because it's going to be about a thirty-minute wait. He goes on to say, "Some of the officers are bringing out inmates to the prison van waiting in the staff parking lot. By morning they'll be transported back to a city near you." So, for thirty minutes eight other people from the outside and I wait while ten inmates are cleared, signed out, and given their papers to leave. Then one by one they are placed inside the prison van.

Each inmate is handcuffed to another inmate so no one can run away. The officer tells us, "What you're seeing folks, are inmates getting ready to go back out on the streets of the Bay Area. They've served their time; they've paid for their crimes, so now it's time to let them go free. The prison gives them a couple of dollars, some street clothes and a ride downtown. Then they're dropped off at some bus station. A few months or maybe a couple of weeks go by and they're usually brought back to San Quentin. It's just a small vacation to them. A little R and R; some time off away from the prison for awhile."

Once I'm inside the prison, I go to the Max Shack and ask for the music class inmate movement sheet. I say hello to the officers, telling them both how glad I am to be back teaching music in the Q. I then open up the music Education Room for class letting in some fresh air.

As I'm taking roll call, in comes one big black lady officer. She walks up the steps, looks at the inmates and then me, and starts barking out the words, "If you're not on the roll call list, then you've got to get the hell out of the building right now!"

Two inmates stand right up, walk past the officer, down the stairs, and out the door. She stands there looking at everyone for about two more minutes, and then leaves not saying another word. It scares the shit out of me having her barking out commands and then watching inmates jumping up and running out of the room when told to leave. Now that is power!

I have six inmates for class. The songs are "Heart Break Hotel" and "The Monster Mash." Everyone plays their hearts out and by the time class ends, they can play and sing both songs. But, just as class is winding down, horns and alarms start going off. Officers are running past the door, yelling out something about a gang fight. As I look out the classroom door, I see inmates sitting down cross-legged on the ground. One of the inmates says, "Look, Buzzy, you just keep teaching the guitar. We all need to just stay inside this room. No one can leave until this shit is over. Don't worry. Boss, this is everyday prison life. It ain't no big deal."

After five minutes of this craziness, everything stops. The officer on duty comes inside the Education Room and says, "Okay, let's roll; it's time to go to bed. Class is over now."

I jump up out of my seat, pack up my guitar and I'm ready to leave in less than two minutes. As I walk back out of the prison, I happen to look up at the officers on the catwalk, guarding the prison. They each have a shotgun and almost look meaner than the inmates. Prison is always a creepy place to work or worse yet, live. I am glad that I can leave, go home to my own little world with my loving family, and my own bed.

Some of the tough boys in the Hall think that I am kidding about the Q. These are young kids who puff out their chest saying things like, "Nothing bothers me. I have to do what I have to do." I've been told the old cons just love the smell of a young fresh fish.

My heart really goes out to these up and coming young badass inmates. It will only take minutes to wipe that smile off their face, once they are behind the walls of San Quentin Prison.

H-Unit One More Time:
Never Say Never

December 7, 1999

It has been nine weeks since I have been in the Q. I'm starting a new class. Never say never. I'm back at H-Unit. Getting inside the Q tonight is easy. Getting inside H-Unit takes a little longer. After waiting for what seems like an hour, I am given the go ahead to be cleared and let inside H-Unit. My escort tells me that nothing is changed in H-Unit. The freaks still bark at the moon and bitch about everything in sight. As soon as the officers and I start walking through the yard, the catcalls start right away, "Hey, Rock Star, hey John, where's Paul? Do you know how to play any Motown, pretty boy?"

After roll call, I have six inmates all ready to learn some songs. The songs tonight are "Santa Claus Is Coming to Town" and "Rockin' Around the Christmas Tree." In the middle of class, one of the inmates shares a story about his childhood. He tells us that when he was a very young boy he had tried to learn how to play the guitar. But he had to hide inside the family's closet with the door shut so that his drunken father wouldn't hear and find him, because his dad would beat him up with the guitar. He goes on to say that his dad hated music and when he drank, he would get really crazy. Somehow the music triggered something bad in his mind. He also told us his dad had died a few years back while he was locked up here in the Q, so he never got the chance to say his last goodbye. He is being released in about sixty days.

He goes on to tell us that he's a two-strikes offender and if he fucks up one more time he'll be looking at life. It ends up being a mellow class for everyone. Christmas in H-Unit, I can hardly wait.

December 21, 1999

Again I have missed the last few weeks of music class because of numerous lock downs. There has been a lot of fighting going on between inmates. As I pull into the east gate entrance, the feeling of Christmas goes away. Having Christmas in prison has got to be hard on the inmates and their families. I'm told by the officer on night watch that the prison staff sometimes allows the kids of inmates a little more contact with their dads around Christmas. Otherwise the children of the inmates in H-Unit have very limited contact with their dads. So at Christmas time, they do this for the kids.

As I wait to be cleared so I can enter the grounds of H-Unit, I watch as the moms and kids of some of the inmates at H-Unit stand in a long line with tears in their eyes. All so their kids can play, hug and kiss their dads for a few minutes over the holidays. I feel very sorry for the children having to see their fathers under these conditions. They are being exposed to a bad and ugly environment. The chances of some of these kids ending up in a prison are pretty high. The officer at H-Unit tells me that the staff would provide some cookies, punch, and a little Christmas tree to make it look more like Christmas.

As I enter the officers' main post, I notice a really big sign hanging on the captain's office window. In big black letters, it reads, "I can only please one person per day. Today is not your day and tomorrow does not look good either." Merry Christmas!

After my escort arrives we head over to the classroom where I am greeted by twelve inmates all ready to sing Christmas songs. It is one of the biggest classes I have had, almost too big. It's a lot of inmates in one room for one music teacher to deal with, but hey, it's Christmas. What can go wrong? It is only prison. So for two hours we sing and play Christmas songs. Everything from "White Christmas" to "Santa Claus Is Coming to Town."

Right about this time a tall black inmate raises his hand and asked if he can sing a solo. I say sure, what song? His reply to me is, "Boss, I want to clean my soul. I want to sing "Silent Night" for the whole class. Is that all right? Would you let me do that?" My eyes fill up with tears as I say, "I would love to hear you sing "Silent Night," my friend. Let's hear it!" So he stands up and sings "Silent Night." It brings us all to tears. It feels like a prayer meeting at a southern Baptist Church. His voice sounds like gold to my ears. After he finishes singing, the inmates all stand up and clap their hands, and say Merry Christmas to one another.

While the inmates are putting away their guitars, some inmate puts a black sock on the table while I am not looking. One of the inmates asks me, "Buzzy, do you know what that is?" I look at the sock and then look back at the inmate saying, "It's a sock, so what."

Then another inmate grins at me and says, "No, boss, it's a catch rag; it's what all of us inmates jerk off in. To catch all of the cum in." By now all the inmates are laughing, giving each other high fives. The inmates at H-Unit love toying with my mind, always testing me. I sometimes feel like their plaything. Their little human toy. I drive home singing Christmas songs, thinking about that damn sock and how much those inmates at H-Unit love seeing that dumb look on my face. I will have to try harder not to fall for their stupid jokes. Merry Christmas, Buzzy.

December 28, 1999

The past year teaching at the Q has been very strange for me. More and more inmates are coming up to me and asking me if they can take the music class. I have been asked a lot lately if I'm that guy everybody is talking about. "Are you the guy everyone calls the Guitar Man?" So I guess my name is floating around in the Q because of the music class. I still don't know if that is a good thing or a bad thing yet.

I have been given the okay to bring in my drummer buddy, Billy, next week. We will both be sitting in with some former students doing a show for the rest of the inmates in H-Unit.

I hope he does not freak out on me when he enters H-Unit. Billy's one of the only musicians I know of, besides the guys in the band, who is willing to go inside of San Quentin Prison and play music for a bunch of inmates. A lot of my friends have been telling me I'm nuts for teaching a music class in San Quentin Prison. I tell them it feels good when I give back and I love the rush of working in a prison. Call me nuts.

My Christmas gift for each of my students tonight was going to be a slice of fruit from my orange tree in my front yard, but the officer at the first check point tells me people from the outside cannot feed the inmates food. The officer says, "Son, if you don't mind, these oranges look pretty damn juicy. Can I have one and maybe one more for the other officer on night duty?" My reply is, "Keep them; they're yours. Enjoy!"

Once inside H-Unit I have six students. The songs for tonight are "Old Man Down the Road" and "Runaway." I have to put on a new set of guitar strings for one of the inmates in class and as I'm fixing his guitar, I pull a quarter out of my right pants pocket, not thinking anything of it. I use the quarter for pressure in getting this part of the guitar fixed. Seeing the quarter in my hand he says, "Wow! a quarter. Brother, I haven't seen a quarter in years. Can I touch it? Can I just feel it one time, boss man?" This inmate's eyes are almost as big as half-dollars. I am at a loss for words.

After fixing his guitar, I let him hold onto the quarter for the rest of the class. He never stops smiling all through class, just holds onto that quarter and sings while rocking back and forth. As the night goes on, one by one, some of the inmates start to open up by sharing their stories with me about their life in prison. One inmate tells me that he has been involved with the penal institution for almost fourteen years. He goes on to say that he has been locked up in San Quentin, since he was nineteen years old. His face lights up when he tells me that his brother is also locked up in San Quentin. This inmate asks me, "Hey Buzzy, how many other brothers do you know that are locked up in the same prison? Pretty cool, don't ya think." What can I say!

Before class is over, I find out that I am the oldest person in the music class. My students' ages range from twenty-one to thirty-six, leaving me to be grandpa by eight years.

Leaving H-Unit tonight I'm told by one of the officers on night patrol that he has just arrived from another prison in upper Northern California called Pelican Bay. He says, "Son, those assholes in Pelican Bay are mean fucking germs. They scared the shit out of me. They're like crazy fucking pirates. A lot of shit goes on up there. San Quentin Prison inmates are all pussies. Most of these inmates would never stand a chance at Pelican Bay." He smiles, "You have a great drive home. I'll see ya next time."

6

Billy the Drummer

December 30, 1999

My good friend Billy and I are coming to the Q tonight to play music with some of my former music students from H-Unit. The staff is letting some of the inmates inside H-Unit put on a little music show for the other inmates. As Billy and I are cleared to go inside H-Unit, I can tell by the look on Billy's face that H-Unit is already starting to get to him. As we are being escorted to the office of the captain on duty, Billy leans over to me and whispers in my ear, "Buzzy, this place is wild. I have never done anything like this before. I already feel a real heavy vibe going on in here. How long before we leave?"

The first time anyone enters H-Unit, it can really be heavy. I lean back over to Billy and whisper, "Billy, we cannot leave H-Unit for the next two and a half hours. Why? Do you have a date tonight or are you going some place?" His face turns white as a ghost and he says, "Holy shit, are you kidding me? This place gives me the willies."

One of the lady officers sitting behind a big desk asks us if we are up to going on a mini tour of H-Unit. I'm feeling pretty brave, so I say sure, why not. Then she looks over at Billy, "How about you, cowboy? Want to go on a ride?" Billy just nods without saying a word. I am starting to wonder if he'll last the whole time.

The lady officer tells us there are four big dormitories in H-Unit. Two hundred inmates are housed in each dorm. She goes on to say that H-Unit has the same problems that exist outside the walls of San Quentin, drugs, rape, prejudice, gang banging, and alcohol; it can all be found in prison. As she walks us past the prison family waiting room, we see six women waiting to be cleared. We are told some girlfriends or wives of the inmates will try to smuggle drugs in by hiding them in their babies' clothes. To love someone in a prison has got to be hard. I can see the pain in these women's faces. I feel so sad for them; it made me want to cry.

As the three of us walk around the dorms of H-Unit, some of the inmates make funny faces at Billy and me. Others are blowing kisses at us, while some inmates just put their fist in the air and yell, "ZZ Top, Rock n' Roll forever!" That lady officer says that for every two hundred inmates there is only one TV set. Not my kind of party. She asks us if we want to go to where the inmates who are really sick with AIDS are housed. We shake our heads and tell her no thanks, maybe the next time around. "We better get over to the inmate dining hall in H-Unit," I tell her. "We have to play some music for the inmates in a little bit; but thank you. Can you please escort us to the dining hall?" As she drops us off, she tells us to enjoy ourselves and be safe. Then she yells, "Take it easy with the musicians, fellows. Don't hurt them. They're here to play some music for you; so don't blow it."

When Billy and I enter H-Unit's dining hall, over seven hundred inmates greet us. Some are standing around talking; others are outside smoking just waiting for the music to begin. When the music starts, the inmates begin dancing and singing at the top of their lungs. As always, to look out and see inmates dancing with each other is shocking. Some of the inmates look like women while others look like bikers. It is really a strange sight. The first group to play is from my first class at H-Unit. They play six songs and sound pretty good. Next up is a folk duo. Both inmates sing and play the guitar. They do songs like "This Land is Your Land." After them, comes a blues band. These inmates have looks on their faces that would kill. They play a couple of Rolling Stones songs and a few other old blues songs. Both Billy and I agree that they rocked.

Then it's our time to entertain. As I plug in my guitar all the inmates start yelling out, "Free Bird" and stomping the floor with their feet. By now the rest of my class has come up and is getting ready to play. With Billy behind the drums, we begin to rock the prison dining hall with "Rock This Town," "I Fought the Law," "Secret Agent Man," "Tush" and, of course, "Free Bird." I catch Billy staring at some of the inmates holding hands and kissing while we play the Temptations' song "My Girl."

About three times I think Billy is going to pass out, but he plays great. He never misses a beat. As it turns out, everything goes very smoothly. The inmates love us. There are no fights; nobody gets hurt. But I'm pretty sure that Billy will never come back to San Quentin any time soon.

As we are being escorted out of H-Unit, an inmate walks up to us and asks, "When I get out next year, can we get together and maybe form a band? What do ya think, boss?" I keep on walking, acting like I don't hear him. Driving home Billy keeps saying, "I can't wait to get home so that I can kiss my wife and my kids. Don't ever ask me to come to this freak show again. It's way too heavy for me. I love you, Buzzy, but San Quentin Prison is a nut farm."

January 4, 2000

There have been a lot of lock downs in the Q, so my music classes have been small. It seems to me that every inmate in H-Unit hates and respects the other inmates at the same time. The whites hate the Mexicans. The blacks hate the whites and the Mexican inmates hate the Korean inmates.

As I'm being escorted into H-Unit tonight an officer on night watch tells me that white people in prison are called "Woods," slang for Peckerwood. "Quiet" cells are padded cells, which are used on loud and unmanageable inmates. The "Balcony" is the check-in wall post for all of the gunner positions. "Pruno" is a very basic manufactured wine that is easy to manufacture in prison. The officer goes on to tell me the inmates in H-Unit have been on a lot of lock downs lately because of the influx of very young gang bangers.

I have three black inmates for class tonight. It's mellow and low key. The songs for class are "Pink Houses" and "Pretty Woman." After an hour of music class, one of the inmates asks me if I knew the difference between the words convict and inmate? I say, "No, what's the difference?" He smiles and says, "Boss, inmates are all the new kids on the block, young guns! These fish have blown it on the outside a little bit too much. Maybe ended up in a County Jail somewhere in California one too many times. Now convicts are old fucks that have been in prison for a long, long time. Most of us have done some hard-core shit to be in prison for this many years. It's all about the years that you spend behind the walls."

Another inmate says, "Some inmates want to stay in prison while others work to get into prison. That is what the goal is to some inmates here in H-Unit." He goes on to say that a lot of these inmates have fathers, brothers, uncles or friends who have been in and out of prison all of their lives. The cycle won't or can't be broken, no matter how hard someone tries. He tells me, "I like this music class so much I want to stay in the Q a little longer. Living on the streets, when it's cold and I'm hungry, sucks. Sleeping in a mission does not thrill me much. Being let out of prison is not always a good thing. Some inmates really like being locked up and being told what to do. It makes their life a lot easier. But I must say the food in prison sucks. A lot of rice with red sauce. It's the main food for dinners. We call it prison slop. The good thing about prison for me is that I don't have to beg in order to eat. The beds in prison are always warm and all of my friends are here in San Quentin. I think I'd feel lost living too long on the outside. That's why a lot of inmates will re-offend so that the judge will send them back to prison. It's like going home for some of us inmates. We've been locked up for so long, we've grown use to it."

Right about this time the other black inmate says, "Okay, girls, I just want to say that I've been really bummed out for the last week. So I decided not to go to my prison job for a few days. I was just too overwhelmed about being locked up in prison for life, and bang, I get fired by my San Quentin boss, plus there's no unemployment from the Q. Life sucks being in this institution."

After class is over, I thank all three inmates and say goodbye. As I'm being escorted back out, I tell the officer on night watch how good the music class went that night. As I drive home I think of something that happened to my soul last week in Juvenile Hall. I was telling some of the boys and girls stories of San Quentin and about teaching a class with inmates in prison, when this little girl about fourteen years old asked me in a really low voice, "Buzzy, if you see my dad in San Quentin, would you tell him that I miss and love him, no matter what." I didn't have the heart to tell her that I didn't know her dad, or where he was housed in the Q. She tells me after class that her father was sent to prison for molesting her and her sister. But, now she forgives him for all the bad stuff he did to them when they were young.

The stories that I have heard from both inmates in prison and the kids in Juvenile Hall are so ugly it brings me to my knees. It tears my heart apart hearing what happens in their lives. And, somehow these kids can still forgive their fathers. Wow! It is very moving for me to be teaching music in these places. Hopefully, music is making a big difference in their lives.

Double Duty:
Teaching Music at the Ranch and
H-Unit

January 11, 2000

Starting this week I will be teaching two music classes at San Quentin. Tuesday nights I will be teaching a class at the "Ranch." On Wednesday nights I will be at H-Unit putting together a prison band. Both classes will last eight weeks.

The Ranch is a kind of holding cage for the inmates that will be getting out of San Quentin within one year. Most inmates at the Ranch are there for non-violent crimes; things like drunk driving, child support delinquency, bad check writing or shop lifting. It's kind of like a mild boot camp for knuckle heads but nevertheless, it's still part of San Quentin State Prison. The Ranch has no cells, no bars; it's almost like summer camp for cons. It feels a lot mellower working at the Ranch than H-Unit, I can tell you that. There are yellow lines painted everywhere around the Ranch. The inmates at the Ranch cannot cross any lines, at any time. Only the officers and staff can cross the lines. Teachers can cross the lines, too. I was told the unspoken rule at the Ranch is to get along with your fellow inmates; otherwise, things will change for you at the snap of a finger.

As I walk into the Ranch tonight, some of the inmates are playing a baseball game. Others are walking around the baseball field, talking to each other or yelling at the inmates across the road in H-Unit.

The main officer on night watch greets me when I arrive and walks me over to the office so I can get my inmate movement sheet (IMS). After checking in, I am shown where the music class will take place. Six inmates are waiting for me; four white inmates, one black inmate, and one little Mexican inmate with no teeth and lots of tattoos, all hungry to learn how to play some music. So for the next two-and-one-half hours, I teach the inmates the songs "Mustang Sally" and "I Feel Good." The class ends on a great note. I can feel a lot of emotions flying around in the Education Room. They are all singing, "I feel good together. So good, so good, I got you."

Brother James Brown would be proud hearing these inmates singing "I Feel Good" in prison. After class each inmate thanks me for coming into the prison and teaching music to them. With handshakes and high fives, I say goodbye to them until next Tuesday night. I wonder how tomorrow's class in H-Unit is going to be, because the Ranch seems to be a cakewalk.

As I drive home all I can think about is how crazy it must be having officers always looking over your shoulder or having other inmates giving you a hard time by toying with your mind. That is got to be really rough on one's soul.

January 12, 2000

It's only been a little over twenty-four hours since I have been at the Ranch. Now I'm driving back to go to H-Unit. Tonight's goal is to start a prison band.

After checking in with the officer on duty, I am told we are going to hold class in the family-visiting unit. The movement sheet has nine names, but only six inmates show up, making it a little easier to show each inmate how to play a song. I find a drum set, three amps, one keyboard, and a full PA with mikes. Everything needed to start a band. The prison staff had some of the inmates bring this stuff down from the North Block just for tonight's class.

So, for the next eight weeks, I am going to try to put these inmates together and see if we can learn to play a couple of songs. It takes me about twenty minutes to hook everything up so that it works. It takes less than one minute for the inmates to jump up on the drums and other stuff. A couple of the inmates who can play the guitar pretty good start playing the Deep Purple song "Smoke on The Water" with the amps turned up to ten. The rest of the inmates in the room rock their heads back and forth while playing their guitars. What a sight. These inmates are like kids on crank. I want to scream "shut up," but decide just to hit the snare drum hard a couple of times. And, just like a room full of little boys, everyone stops, looks at me and then sits down. Once everyone has calmed down, I teach the inmates the songs "Susie Q," "Born to Be Wild," and "Stormy Monday." Three inmates raise their hands to ask if they can sing any one of the songs. So I split up the songs, one for each inmate. One of the inmates who wants to sing is black with three gold teeth. He wears a headband and sunglasses the whole time, so I never see his eyes. The other inmate who wants to sing is a white skinhead with a shaved head and tattoos everywhere, plus he is missing some of his teeth. But I must say, this inmate sings like Bon Scott, the first lead singer of the band AC/DC. So, I give him the song "Born to Be Wild" to sing. The last inmate who wants to sing is Mexican. This inmate has a floating eye and he smiles all the time. He asks if he can sing the song "Susie Q." For the next two and one-half hours, we work on all three songs. No pee breaks, I keep things moving at a pretty fast pace; otherwise, the inmates get bored really quick.

As it works out, everyone has a pretty good time. After class is over and I am driving home, my head hurts and my ears ring from all the noise. I think that for the next seven weeks I will bring some earplugs in with me; otherwise, my hearing is going to be shot. If someone had told me that some day I would be putting together a band of inmates in a prison, I would have thought that he was crazier than a loon. Never say never!

April 4, 2000

I have had a lot of time off due to lock downs. There has been lots of gang fighting going on inside the prison. It seems to be over control and power rights. I'm told by one of the officers that there is one top dog for every race. One black top dog, one white top dog, one Mexican top dog; they all have their own top dog and no inmate ever fucks with those top dogs, ever. That is the golden rule in prison, if you want to get along and stay out of trouble while being locked up.

It is so strange for me to see nice old houses with dogs and kids playing in the front yards, all within three hundred yards of the prison. There are a couple of streets with rows of 1950's style homes that look like they are right out of a movie. I'm sure the families living in these houses must have a story or two to tell about living so close to San Quentin Prison.

The Ranch is so mellow. The Ranch is like a cakewalk, not much stress; a bunch of inmates just watching the time go by. The songs for tonight are "Folsom Prison Blues" and "Jailhouse Rock." One of the inmates tells me that he plays the guitar for sometimes up to eight hours a day.

The class runs very smoothly. No inmates give me a hard time. I must say that the inmates in the Ranch are the easiest to deal with and the inmates locked up in H-Unit are by far the creepiest inmates that I've worked with.

As I drive home, I think about the kids I'm going to see tomorrow morning in Juvenile Hall. I wonder how many of those kids will end up living their lives out behind the walls of San Quentin Prison. Most of the kids that I work with look up to other gang members that have been locked up in a prison (their role models). It gives them status among up and coming fellow gang members. Most feel coming into an institution like San Quentin is no big deal. Thank God, the music class at the Ranch was very low key tonight. I sure hope that it stays this way for all of the classes.

April 5, 2000

Last week in H-Unit was pretty damn crazy. My ears rang for two days because of the amps turned up to ten by the inmates. So, tonight I'm wearing earplugs and bringing in my own amp because I could not hear myself on the guitar at all last week but now I will. Sixty watts of power, just enough, so my guitar won't get lost in the mix.

Being escorted into H-Unit tonight I am reminded right away of the bad vibes from some of the inmates. Again tonight I hear all the catcalls. Things like, "Where's Mick Jagger?" or "Hey, Rock Star, do you play requests?" It's never gotten any easier for me having big hard ass inmates blowing me kisses. The thing that freaks me out the most is when an inmate asks me questions about my family or where I live.

For the most part, H-Unit music class has not been that bad; it's getting to the room that is the hardest part. And leaving the building is not much better. After being let into the conference room, I set up everything, as an officer looks on not saying one word to me the whole time. The inmates are let into the room one at a time. I teach the inmates the songs "Bad to the Bone" and "Hit the Road Jack." I must say it sounds good, really good! The inmates in class get along great, never using any bad words or fighting with each other. Another example of how music civilizes these inmates, for a little while at least. It seems to be their safe place so they can just be themselves for a couple of hours without getting messed with by other inmates. The song "Bad to the Bone" is a big hit with the class. Each inmate takes his turn singing the song by himself. We play "Bad to the Bone" six times. By the time we get to the sixth time, it sounds great.

When the officer comes back to unlock the door, he tells us that for a bunch of jerk-offs, we didn't sound too bad. He goes on to say, "Maybe if you girls work real hard, you can get yourself a paying gig opening for the Rolling Stones."

I stop by the officers' main post to say goodbye and turn in my paperwork when an officer looks at me and yells, "Goddamn, what the hell are you doing in here, son? I've seen you on TV and I've read about you in the newspaper." Then he looks at the other officer on duty and says, "Hey, Bob, this guy is famous. He works with a lot of kids at risk. He teaches them music. He gives them a little love and understanding so that they won't end up here with the rest of the misfits."

What an odd cartoon prison is. I'm not sure how much longer I can work in this place. It's starting to get inside my mind. I can't even wear blue jeans on my days away from the prison any more, and that is nuts. I should write a book about teaching a music class inside of San Quentin Prison. I wonder if anyone would read it.

April 19, 2000

Having two classes a week in the Q is making me nuts. I'm starting to get burned out a little faster than I thought I would. It's getting to be way too much for my brain to handle. I could not work forty hours a week in the Q. I would have a breakdown. Pain and hopelessness must grow behind the walls of San Quentin like cancer. The thing about life in a prison is having so much time on your hands to do nothing. I hope I can finish all eight weeks of classes without flipping out.

As I pull my truck into the staff parking lot, it begins to rain pretty hard. By the time I reach H-Unit, I am soaked. Checking in tonight, I'm told by my escort that life around H-Unit has been pretty nutty lately. I end up with nine students. Everyone has his turn pounding on the drums or playing the guitar. After what seems like years, I teach the inmates the songs "Great Balls of Fire" and "My Girl." The black inmate with the gold teeth sings "My Girl" while the white skinhead inmate sings "Great Balls of Fire."

After two hours of hacking away at these songs, the inmates sound like a pretty good bar band. Three of the inmates try to make up dance steps like the Temptations while Mr. Skinhead sings "My Girl."

As the class comes to a close, one of the Mexican inmates thanks me for letting him take out his anger by hitting on the drums. He also tells me it really helps him to be playing music while he's locked up. He goes on to say that music makes these inmates forget they're in prison for a while. Another inmate tells me he only has four more weeks left in H-Unit and then he's free. "Boss, this is it. I hope that I don't fuck up while I'm out this time. I really don't want to come back to this hellhole." And then he holds up his right hand showing me a silver pinkie ring with a skull on it. "On behalf of all the other inmates and myself, we're very glad for everything you've done for us in H-Unit. You're a good guy, Buzzy. We all trust you because you don't judge us. We respect you because you respect us; and so I want to give you this skull ring to remember us when you are on the outside. So here it is; take it. It's yours." And with that, he takes off the ring and hands it to me.

I say thank you to him and put it on my finger. I can tell that the mood is changing between us. As I'm being escorted back out of H-Unit, a couple of skinhead inmates start barking at me like junkyard dogs. After a couple of howls, one of the inmates asks me, "Hey, boss, is it possible to teach us how to play some of that fag rock n' roll; you know, like that shit on MTV where the guys look like sluts." And then he starts laughing, telling me to go fuck myself.

When I returned to my truck the first thing I did was take off the skull ring and put it inside my coat pocket. After driving home and talking to my wife, we both decided it would be better to put the ring away in a drawer and never wear it again.

Thank God I can leave and go home to my own bed and bathroom. All in all a very mellow night in H-Unit except for me accepting the skull ring as a gift from the inmate.

April 25, 2000

I have missed the last two Tuesday nights at the Ranch due to a couple of fights between inmates. The staff put the inmates at the Ranch on lock down for twenty-four hours that calmed everyone down. I feel a little bad for the inmates in the music class because they count on me so much to come into the Q and teach the class.

Some inmates get really pissed off at the prison staff if music class is called off. The officer at the east gate tells me that the inmates at the Ranch are waiting for their dose of music. It has been too long. They are starting to bitch like little girls.

Once I arrive at the Ranch and take roll call, I have five inmates for class. The songs for tonight are "Hound Dog" by Elvis and the Blues Brothers' song "Shotgun Blues." The nights at the Ranch run so smoothly, I sometimes forget I am in a prison. At ten minutes to nine I ask the class, "How long can we play music tonight? Do we have to stop at nine?"

One of the inmates looks at the rest of the class and back at me with a grin, "Buzzy, you can stay here till ten o'clock or even all night if you really want to. We've got a couple of extra beds and some clothes in your size. You can have some chow in the morning. What do ya think, boss, do ya want to stay overnight and hang with the boys at the Ranch or what?"

My reply is, "Great, how's the room service?" After everyone stops laughing an officer comes into the room to say that class is over and bed check is in ten minutes. As I walk to my truck, the shadows of the officers walking on the catwalk dance on the rain soaked streets of the grounds. Teaching music in a prison has got to be the wildest thing that I have ever done.

April 26, 2000

Coming into H-Unit as much as I have, I find it never gets any easier for me. It still makes my heart skip a beat every so often, unlike the Ranch I am always escorted wherever I go while I'm in H-Unit.

I can never walk freely around the yard or any of the buildings in H-Unit. The inmates in H-Unit are having another showcase tonight and I'm playing some songs with a couple of my former students. It should be a blast. As I sign in tonight I can again hear the words, "The Guitar Man is here," blasting over the prison PA speakers.

While I wait for my escort to arrive, the officer behind the desk keeps smiling at me and then says, "A couple of the other officers around here told me that you're a rock star. Is that true, are you famous?" I smile back at the officer and say, "I have been playing a few high profile concerts around the Bay Area to help raise some money for the music programs for kids at risk; so lately I have been getting my share of press; things like TV and newspapers. Which means my face is all over the Bay Area." I also tell the officer, "I have had inmates asking me things like, didn't I see you on TV before or didn't I read about you in the newspaper just last week?" I tell the officer I am just a guitar player, singer who has had a little luck along the way, so now I'm giving back by helping others through music.

My escort asks me if I am ready to go to the dining hall because the inmates are waiting for me, so that they can start the show. With that said he opens up the door and says, "Let's roll, my friend, it's time to go."

The music shows are always in the inmate dining hall. This place must hold six hundred inmates easy. When I walk inside the dining hall, all the drums and amps are set up and there must be five hundred inmates just hanging around. I am told that there are five different acts in the show tonight and we are one of them.

The first group has four inmates who play be-bop jazz. They have an old black guy who sings and plays guitar. The bass player is Mexican and the drummer is a big white tattooed skinhead with two front teeth missing. They play four songs that sound pretty good. I like them; but the inmates do not seem to like the jazz too much. After every song, some inmate yells out something like, "I hate this fag music," or "what the hell are you assholes trying to play?"

The next act is a trio: bass, guitar and drums. The bass player sings all of the songs. They play four head-banging songs at one thousand miles an hour. None of them smile. The guitar player spits out chew every few minutes in between solos. I must say they are much better than the inmate jazz band. The last song played is "Smoke on the Water" by Deep Purple at full volume. Then it is our turn. We decide to do "Bad to the Bone," "Shotgun Blues," "Hound Dog" and the ZZ Top song "Tush."

We go over pretty good. Thank God no inmates yell anything at me. After our set is over, two inmates sing campfire songs, things like "On Top of Old Smokey" or "I've Been Working on the Railroad." About 8:30 p.m. the last act comes on up. Five inmates who all sing, three black inmates, one white and one really short Mexican inmate with a glass eye. No one plays an instrument. It's like hearing the Temptations, only without any music. Their vocals are great and they even have the Motown moves, turning from side to side. The other inmates are eating it up. They are just loving it! They sing three songs, but what great songs: "My Girl," "Tears of a Clown," and ending with "Amazing Grace," in five-part harmony. It blows us away. When they stop singing, the inmates stand up and cheer for one more. I am right there cheering for them too. They sing one last song, ending the showcase with "Over the Rainbow" from the Wizard of Oz.

It is very sad that none of these inmates can ever show off their music skills outside of the walls of the Q. I wish I could take some pictures or could have recorded some of the inmate performances to show people outside the prison. I have never thought of musicians as outlaws, but I am sure other people may differ with me. I have found that there are some pretty good musicians in the Q.

After the showcase is over and I'm putting away my guitar, one of my former guitar students walks up to me and says, "Hey, boss, how are ya doing? I just thought that I'd come back again and get a couple more guitar lessons in. It's been over a year. I've missed ya, bro. I've missed the old place, so here I am. Find out if there's room for me in your next class. I'm going to be locked up again for awhile."

I would think that one time being locked up in a prison would be more than enough; but for some reason these inmates in H-Unit just cannot get enough of the prison life. As if that was not strange enough, another inmate comes up and introduces himself and his brother. He says they have both been locked up in the Q for about five years. He tells me "My bro and me are family. No one can ever break that bond. If anyone ever fucks with my bro, I'll kill them. That's my law." Both of these inmates are very buffed out, with lots of tattoos. Both smell of cheap cigarettes and lots of body odor. After a few minutes of talking, we say our good-byes and I slap each inmate a high five.

Driving out of the Q tonight, I can smell the Bay water in the air. I can also hear the sweet sounds of birds singing to each other while sitting on the east gate wall. What a contrast to prison life. The bay on the left side and San Quentin Prison on the right side. The land of incarceration. A city of dead souls living in the town of pain.

I wish I could bring in a bunch of these kids from the Hall and drop them off for a weekend. I hope it would freak them out enough so they would stay out of trouble.

June 6, 2000

I'm at the Ranch tonight and tomorrow night I'm back at H-Unit. Then I will be taking off three months for the summer. Time away from San Quentin is much needed. As I pull my truck into the staff parking lot, I can hear the horns blowing and see blue lights flashing inside H-Unit. There are officers running around yelling as the inmates begin sitting down. As I turn my head, I can see a lot of the inmates at the Ranch involved in a baseball game. Not one inmate at the Ranch seems to give a shit about what is going on at H-Unit.

The night officer at the Ranch tells me "The inmates are going to miss you. They look forward to the music class every week. It makes them forget they're in prison for a little bit. It also helps calm them down when they become mad over being locked up in the Q for so long. Plus it is a time killer."

When the officer opens up the door of the Education Room, a blast of hot air comes pouring out, so he tells me to keep the door open all night. One by one the inmates walk in. I can tell by the look on their faces that they are going to miss the music class. After roll call, I tune their guitars, and then show them "Lean on Me" and "Rocky Mountain Way." The two hours fly by really fast and for some reason every inmate sings his butt off. When the class comes to an end, I am given a handmade card signed by all the inmates at the Ranch. The card reads, "Thank you, Buzzy, for bringing sunshine into a really dark day. Thanks for the music, signed all the students at the Ranch, San Quentin Prison." I am speechless. All I can say is thank you from the bottom of my heart.

While I'm putting away my guitar, two students tell me the music classes have helped them build up their self-esteem and made them care about something other than a life of crime.

I am always reminded of how lucky I'm to have a great family and a home. I understand the meaning of the word freedom. It is a word that I will never take for granted now that I have seen other men without it.

June 7, 2000

H-Unit will be my last music class for the summer. I'm taking a little time off to rest my brain. Coming into San Quentin two times a week is getting to be too much. My body is starting to feel toxic. I need a break from the prison. A couple of months away to clean out my soul.

Walking into H-Unit tonight I find my heart is racing a little faster. Maybe because it's my last night. I ask the officer behind the desk how long he has worked at San Quentin. He looks at me for what seems like hours and finally says, "I've been working here for ten long years, son. I can't wait till I can retire. This place is a fucking zoo. How long have you been coming to San Quentin?" Just then my escort showed up putting an end to our conversation. As we walk through the yard, everything is calm, inmates walking around or playing basketball, nothing like last night.

For the next two hours, I teach my class the songs "Twist and Shout," "Smoke on the Water" and "Long Tall Sally." At times the music and the inmates get pretty crazy with everyone trying their hand at singing, thumping on the bass guitar or banging on the drums. We come together quickly as a class, almost sounding as good as a bar band and sometimes even better.

At ten minutes to nine we are told by one of the biggest officers I have ever seen that music class is over. He tells the class to put away everything and get in line as fast as their feet will carry them.

After a few minutes he barks, "Get in line and get ready to move out because bed check is in fifteen minutes." As we march down the hallway carrying our guitars I remember I have forgotten my picks back in the room. So without thinking, I turn around and go back. But when I return to be let out, no one is around. The door is locked and everything is dark. I am trapped like a fat rat in prison. The silence is deafening. All I can hear is the sound of me breathing really hard. I can now feel the sweat starting to run down my face. I have to bang on that door for what feels like over three hours, but couldn't have been any more than three or four minutes. The thought of losing my freedom makes me pound on the door even harder. I then start to yell at the top of my lungs, "Help me, I'm locked in here. Please let me out, help!" I start to laugh to myself, how stupid is this, that I got myself locked in an office inside of San Quentin prison and nobody can hear me yelling. Just then I hear the sounds of footsteps and keys swinging from side to side. As the officer opens up the door, I can smell the sweet scent of fresh air. While I wipe away the sweat from my face, the officer barks at me, "Where in the hell did you run off to? You just disappeared on me. I have been looking for you for about five minutes. We need to know where everyone is at all times in the prison. That way if there is a riot or a lock down everyone is covered. That kind of shit can get you in big trouble with the staff. Do not ever do that again. Do you understand, son?" All I can say is, "Yes sir, can I go home now?"

Except for those few minutes, tonight was very mellow. I will not miss this place for the three months that I'm off.

As I drive out of the east gate, I stop my truck and say, "Good night San Quentin Prison. I will see ya in three months. Take care!" Driving home feels great, knowing I am going to get some rest. I wonder where I will be teaching when I return in September.

Back in North Block, Again

September 12, 2000

This is my first night back after three months away. I'm coming back to teach at North Block. My boss tells me that I now have an inmate aid. He will help me with my class, assist with the other inmates, take care of all my paperwork, and other tasks if I need him to.

As I drive into the parking lot, I can feel the prison vibe right away. It only takes me one minute before that creepy feeling comes rushing back with the big bang of the steel prison door slamming behind me. I am welcomed back to the penitentiary by some of the officers on duty. The prison smell is pretty thick tonight. Nothing has changed in the Q except for the date. An officer tells me that last Sunday all of San Quentin was on lock down for all white inmates. Today, it's the black inmates on lock down, so it could be a very lightly attended class.

Looking at my inmate movement sheet I am shocked to see that I have fourteen inmates signed up for music class. For the next sixteen weeks, I will be coming into the main unit. This is my biggest class ever in the three years I have been teaching music at the prison. I am really happy to be back where I first started teaching music.

The North Block is not as fucked up as H-Unit. So this should be a great class. When I arrive at the Max Shack I'm greeted by an inmate who tells me that he is my new teacher's aid. He has a great big smile on his face. He wears thick glasses and is very nice, telling me whatever I need he will get for me: pens, paper, copies of songs, anything. "You can tell me what to do and bang, it's done. I'm yours for the next sixteen weeks. You call the shots and I'll dance for ya, boss."

It is a little strange to have an inmate to help me. I'm sure that my new aid will work out fine, but it's still a strange feeling.

For the next few minutes, inmates from every ethnic group in the Q except for blacks come to the music class. One of the white inmates tells me, "Hey boss, all the blacks are on lock down; it's their turn to kick it up in the Q."

While I'm talking to this inmate, another inmate walks into the room. He looks like a wise guy straight out of a Mafia movie. His hair is greased straight back and he talks like he's from New Jersey. The first thing he says is, "Yo, I respect any fucking musician that comes to a prison and teaches music to the inmates. You got some big balls. Can you teach me how to play the blues? I'm a lifer. I ain't ever getting out. I killed a guy with a baseball bat; smacked him right in the back of his fucking head. Pow! He never knew what hit him. But his buddy sure did and that's why I'm in here. That's my fate, to die in this place. So, I thought maybe music would be a good thing to learn. Otherwise, I'm doing nothing but waiting to die, or getting into bad moods all of the time. Playing the guitar sounds like a much better choice. Plus it'll keep my mind busy instead of thinking about how lonesome my heart is being locked up in the Q."

My aid tells me that six of my students are lifers, with no hope of ever getting out. After roll call is over I find out which inmates can play the guitar and which knew nothing about music. I'm happy to learn that half of the class can already play some songs on the guitar. The other half should catch on pretty quickly. All these inmates have is time to practice. I teach the class two songs. "What I Say" by Ray Charles and "House of the Rising Sun." I give all of the inmates copies of the chords and music to both songs. As I am teaching the inmates the words to "What I Say," the door swings open and in walks a six-foot, four-inch, two hundred and eighty pound black officer pointing his finger at me. He stops and says in a low voice with a Jamaican accent, "Hello, mun. I'm Jamaican, and

I need to ask you a couple of questions, mun. I want to play the guitar. Where can I buy one cheap in the Bay Area and how much will it cost me, mun?"

So for five minutes, I tell the officer about prices of guitars and where to go to buy one. He smiles and thanks me, "Straight up, mun." Just as he walks out, shutting the door behind him, all hell breaks loose, with alarms going off, buzzers ringing and the sound of officer's boots running, with their keys swinging back and forth against their belts.

I can hear an officer saying something about an inmate fight breaking out in the dining hall. The next thing that I hear is, each inmate starting to howl the same note as the alarms going off. What a picture. Grown men acting like lost little puppies with no identity, no hopes, and no future.

My aid leans over and says, "Hey boss, this happens all the time around here. Ain't no big deal; everyday prison life. Unless you start hearing guns going off, there's no worries." He is right! After about ten minutes of yelling and craziness, outside the Education Room, everything just stops like nothing has happened. Within one minute all of the inmates go right back to playing their guitars and singing. I find that there is little difference between prison and Juvenile Hall, except in prison, some staff have guns! After two-and-one-half hours of having way too much fun, I have to call it a night.

While everyone is putting away their guitars, I explain to the inmates about the music class I do with kids at risk in the Juvenile Hall. I ask them if they had a chance to say something to a couple of these little gang bangers I work with, what would they say to these kids who tell me "Prison ain't shit. I can handle myself. Prison will be cool. Don't worry about me." "Any words of wisdom for these knuckleheads?"

One of the inmates stops what he is doing and looks me straight in the eyes. "Buzzy, those boys would be eaten alive within days of getting to the Q. Nothing better than some fresh fish for dinner. You go back and tell those young smart ass kids that, unless they like having sex with some old smelly cons or always looking over their shoulder, or having officers always barking, telling you how to live your life they will be sleeping with one eye open. This is no place for a child. Tell them to just stay in school. The prison life is two degrees shy of hell. You will do things in prison that are unthinkable. How's that, Buzzy? Does that answer your question about what to say to the kids?"

My reply is, "Wow!" At 9:00 p.m. sharp, two officers came to say that inmate bed check is in ten minutes. So all of the inmates have to hurry; otherwise they would get in trouble with the staff.

As I am walking past the prison church, I can hear the sweet sounds of the inmates' choir singing "Oh, Happy Day." It's good to be back at the main unit. I don't really want to go back to teach at H-Unit or the Ranch again. I feel much safer working up at North Block.

The inmates in this class are a little bit older, twenty-eight to fifty. Most of the inmates coming into the prison now are very young, eighteen to twenty years old. Three hundred new inmates have been admitted in just the last six months. Welcome back to prison.

9

Crazy Times at the Q

October 24, 2000

The last four weeks have been a bit crazy inside San Quentin. In the last month there has been one execution, four lock downs and two officers have been beaten up by the inmates. San Quentin has been getting a lot of bad press in the news and it's starting to make my wife worry about my safety while I'm inside. She keeps telling me that she is worried something might happen to me while I'm teaching the inmates music. I have told her over and over not to worry, that everything will be fine. I have been teaching music to inmates at San Quentin Prison for a little over three years now and I am very lucky not to have witnessed any drama in class.

Walking in tonight I can feel that the vibe is bad with both officers and the inmates. Once class starts, everything mellows out though. The songs for class are "The Monster Mash" and "Stand By Me." While I'm teaching one of the inmates how to play "Stand By Me," he starts barking at me. "Look boss, I'm having a really fucked-up week. I've been locked up in San Quentin for the last fifteen years. I'm a lifer. I'm never getting out of here. I've screwed up my life forever. Now that's a bad space to be in; and the worst part is I will never see my family ever again. My mom, dad, wife, and kids won't come in here to see me. They write me and tell me that because I broke their hearts and trust, I now have to live with that pain for the rest of my life here in San Quentin."

In between songs another inmate talks about how he ended up in prison. He says to us, "It started out with me being asked to drive a car down to the border of California and Mexico for $10,000 cash, a little drugs and no questions asked. Can I do the job;

of course I can, I tell them. So while I was driving this car down to the border, flying down Highway 101 in the middle of the night, I found a 357 gun tucked under the driver's seat. Not thinking any one would hear me fire off a couple of rounds, I shot the gun a few times from the car window; and son of a bitch, someone did hear and called 911. The police set up a roadblock ten miles ahead of me; so when I pulled over I had fifteen or twenty cops pointing guns at my head. When the cops opened up the trunk of the car that I was driving I was shocked to see the body of the owner of the car. He was tied up and smelled pretty bad. After the police had handcuffed me and read me my rights, I tell them that I was set up; that I'm being framed. They had the wrong guy. I'm now doing twenty-five to life in San Quentin Prison just for getting a bit greedy, stupid, and having a really bad lawyer. If something sounds too good to be true; then it is. No one wants to end up living in prison, sleeping in a cage with two other inmates with cells so small, you can only dream of freedom. The one thing in prison that sucks the most is waiting. Waiting in line to eat, waiting to take a shower, waiting to use the phone, or the bathroom. Everyone waits in prison. That's the life of the inmate here in the Q."

Another inmate stands up, "There's cons out on the streets right now that can't wait to be put back into prison. This is our home away from home. Sometimes it's easier just to be a number; don't talk back; and always follow the rules; never try to piss off anybody. Just do the time."

After spending most of the night teaching the inmates the songs "The Monster Mash" and "Stand By Me," I can tell that some of the inmates just want to talk and tell me their stories of prison life. Right at 8:30 p.m. sharp one of the lady officers opens up the door and yells out, "Last call for dinner. The prison is going on a lock down at any moment." Sure enough, horns start going off and lights begin flashing.

The lady officer points her finger at me and yells, "Pick up all your shit right now. Don't run, but come with me and hurry." When I walk outside the Education Room, I feel like I am in a movie.

As I'm being escorted back out of the prison, I am told that for the last couple of hours everything has been getting crazy, inmates fighting with each other and giving the prison staff a lot of shit, so the prison is going on lock down right now.

When we get to the 4 Post by the east gate, the officer's eyes behind the desk get as big as moons when he sees me. He yells, "What the hell are you still doing in here, son? We're in a major lock down. There's a riot going on right this minute. Now sign out and go home."

Leaving the prison tonight is very tense. As I look into my rear view mirror, for the first time I see an officer locking up the big steel gates of San Quentin behind me as I drive off. I can hear the horns blaring in the air as the cold wind blows into my truck window. What a strange adventure. I wonder if my wife is right about my safety.

November 7, 2000

I've been asked about Death Row and if I have ever seen any Death Row inmates. I can't enter the Death Row unit because it's off limits to most staff, but I have heard some pretty horrible stories about what happens between inmates and officers there. It sounds way too negative for my heart. The inmates sitting on Death Row have done some really bad things. No nice inmates on that unit.

As I enter San Quentin's main courtyard, one of the inmates gives me a thumbs up and a smile. When I get close enough to say hi, he starts singing, "Papa Was a Rolling Stone" while he dances. I have seen some pretty crazy things in my lifetime, but having an inmate singing and dancing for me in a prison is way over the edge. After two minutes of watching this old black inmate dance and sing, I tell him I have to go, but to keep up the good work with his singing.

When I arrive at the Education Room, I have eight inmates waiting for music class to begin. There must be over three hundred inmates walking around outside. Some are going to dinner or class or just walking back to their cells.

After roll call is over I ask the inmates if I can teach them the songs "Rock This Town" and "Jailhouse Rock." Just then, this short inmate from Indonesia looks at me and then at each inmate. He says dreamily with something of an accent, "The Stray Cats and Elvis. Elvis, King of Wock and Woll. His voice sound like gold to me. Everyone sing his songs."

I am floored at his knowledge of American classic rock n' roll music. He goes on to tell me that I can ask him anything about rock n' roll music and he would probably know the answer. So for ten minutes I ask him questions about the Beatles, Jerry Lee Lewis, ZZ Top and Elvis! He is right! He knows all the answers. The rest of the class just sits there cheering him on. We are all impressed. Afterwards he stands up on a chair and takes a bow, saying thank you about ten times and grinning from ear to ear.

He tells us he has been in prison for nine years and all he does is listens to old classic rock n' roll. "I wuv living in USA. I wuv wock music and I wuv contwee music. It help to get me through another day in prison."

His smile fades away, he looks me straight in the eyes and says, "I kill a man with a pipe. I hit him five time before he fell down and die. That guy was in wong place at wong time. I fuck up. I feel sowwy for his family but it too late for me. I'm lifer. That why I wuv music so much. It take my mind off of pain I cawwy for killing that guy for no fucking good reason."

At this point another inmate tells me, "I've got a story for you and your kids in the Hall. I killed a man with a knife. He got me real pissed off. I was having a real bullshit day and he starts smiling at me and it freaked me out. It just hit me the wrong way. The next thing I know I'm sticking him in the fucking neck with a knife. I kind of felt bad about it, but what can I do. It happened so fast that it was over in just a minute. I ran but I got caught. I wish I could turn back time, make it all change, make it better but that's never going to happen. I'm a lifer, too. I'm never going to leave this prison alive. Tell the kids you work with to stay the hell out of trouble, do their homework, don't quit school, listen to their mom and dad, and don't do drugs. Just be good kids. Don't end up here in prison with the rest of us misfits."

My aid turns to me and says, "Boss, we all respect you for coming into the prison and teaching us music. You're one hell of a guy." Each inmate shakes my hand and says thanks for teaching them some music.

I wonder what kind of childhood these inmates had growing up. What made them so mean and crazy about life? What killed their souls?

November 14, 2000

I wonder how long I can go on doing this prison gig. The last few times I have come into the Q, there has been a lot of fighting going on between inmates. There has also been a lot of news coverage about overcrowding in San Quentin. The prison is old and very unsafe for both the staff and the inmates.

After signing in and getting my inmate movement sheet, I'm told by the officer on night watch duty that all of the white inmates are on lockdown again tonight. He goes on to say, "If you're a black, brown or a yellow-skinned inmate, music class is open for you tonight. If you're a white inmate, you're fucked!"

I have seven inmates show up for class: four blacks, two Mexican, and the Indonesian inmate who knows almost everything about rock music. The class runs very smoothly. We go over a few songs that are easy to do like "Old Time Rock n' Roll," "Jailhouse Rock" and "I Feel Good." It's cool hearing all of the inmates singing the words "so good, so good, I got you."

When music class ends, everyone is laughing and slapping each other high fives. Everyone feels great about the whole night. As we are walking out of the Education Room, one of the inmates turns to say good night to me. Bang! Without any warning, buzzers and alarms start going off, blue flashing lights start scanning from side to side, just like in the movies; only this is all too real. By now officers are running everywhere as every inmate in sight sits down wherever they are.

It's wild for me to see this going on, so I sit down too. Just then, one of my music students whispers to me, "Hey Buzzy, if I were you I would get my ass right up now; but not too fast. I wouldn't sit down here any longer." Slowly I stand back up, but don't move. I think I am in shock. Right then about twenty-five officers in padded vests come running past me. They are all carrying billy clubs and dressed in full riot gear, including black helmets with full-face shields. No one is saying a word as they run past me. I think I am going to shit my pants.

It is hard to hear because of the alarms going off. I freeze this moment in time in my mind, wondering what's going to happen next. Then I feel a tap of someone's finger touching my shoulder. When I turn around, I am facing two big officers. One of the officers tells me to follow him; that he will escort me out of this mess. He says to me, "Son, don't say a word. Just walk with me as fast as your feet will carry you and don't look back."

I do what that officer tells me to do. I just walk as fast as I can and never say one word. Once we have entered the 4 Post by the east gate exit, the officer explains to me that I had come very close to being in the middle of a Stage One lock down. This officer says to me, "You're very lucky to be going home tonight, my friend. All hell's about to break loose in here. If I were you, I'd hop in your truck and get the hell out of Dodge. I've got to go back to work. You be safe driving home and you might want to call in next week to be sure everything's okay here in the Q."

Driving back home with my ears ringing because of the alarms and buzzers going off, I have a funny feeling that when I tell my wife what happened tonight, she is not going to be too pleased about me being caught in the middle of a lock down. Lord, wish me luck next week when I come back to teach the inmates music.

10.

Another Christmas in San Quentin

December 6, 2000

It has been a few weeks since I have taught music at the Q because of lots of lock downs. Things seem to be getting worse.

I must have waited inside the Education Room for at least twenty minutes. One by one, inmates begin to file into class. It's a very small class, only six inmates. I tell the class that tonight's songs will be "Rudolph the Red-Nosed Reindeer" and "Santa Claus Is Coming to Town." I think with Christmas on its way, these songs would be great to learn. The Indonesian inmate knows almost all of the Christmas songs recorded in the last forty-five years here in the United States. He tells me he just loves the Elvis song "Blue Christmas" and Bing Crosby's "White Christmas."

About halfway through the music class one of the inmates raises his hand and asks me if he can say something. I say, "Sure, what's on your mind?" He stands up and says, "Buzzy, all I want for Christmas is to see my boys. They are ten, twelve, and fifteen. I hope to get paroled in the next five years or less. My kids write me, but they won't come to San Quentin to see me. I pray for my sons all the time. I'm a changed man. Once I leave prison this time, I will never come back to the Q. I love my family way too much. Knowing how much pain I brought to my wife and sons kills me inside. I hate this feeling of hurting the people who love me so much." It makes me sad to hear him. I hope he makes it.

The rest of the night goes very smoothly, almost too smoothly! So much has happened at San Quentin in the last thirty days. It's really strange when things are so quiet around the Q. I thank all of the inmates for helping me get through the mini-lock down a few weeks ago. One of the inmates says, "Hey Buzzy, it's eighteen years of experience being in prison. It ain't no big deal. That's what we're here for, to kind of be your tour guides."

All the inmates wish me a Merry Christmas and a happy holiday. Each inmate shakes my hand and says good night. When I walk past the Max Shack both officers wave to me and wish me a happy Christmas, too. As I make my way back to the east gate, I can see Christmas lights in the windows of the prison offices.

I have been told by staff that some of the inmates housed at San Quentin are used to having Christmas in prison. It has become their life. Other inmates are especially mad at the whole world for their own fuck-ups at this time of year so they beat up on everyone because of their own bad choices.

When the officer on night duty opens up the gates to let me out of the prison, he smiles at me and says, "Have a wonderful, Merry Christmas, my friend. Till I see you again, take care and have a great holiday."

Christmas in San Quentin is a sad song. Maybe I will write a song or two about teaching music in prison.

December 27, 2000

It is cold and raining pretty hard. I have missed the last three weeks at the Q due to lock downs again. I am sure glad Christmas has passed because it made me feel sad.

Five inmates show up for class. The songs are "Summertime Blues" and "Brown-Eyed Girl." I could not have asked for a better class. The inmates respect each other and they are learning how to get along as a group. A couple of them have been teaching some of the others how to sing and play the guitar at the same time. I am told that when I'm not here to teach the class, some of the inmates still get together and play music with each other.

One of my students tells me that over Christmas time a lot of the older inmates make toys and other gifts for the kids of other inmates. He says the prison threw a little party for the families of the inmates and he got to play the part of Old Saint Nick. He says that kids were everywhere, laughing, crying or just running around with other inmates' kids. Most of the inmates' wives were very happy just to have their families together even for a few moments at Christmas time. He says no matter what, the children have to see their daddies at Christmas time.

He starts moving his head from side to side, shouting, "Ho, ho, ho, Merry Christmas boys and girls; ho ho ho! That's what I sounded like, not bad for a skinny old white inmate. The children really thought I was Santa."

I am touched. It makes me want to cry.

When I walk back to my truck, the rain splashes on my feet. The sound of a foghorn blows low notes in the winter air, sending sounds through the wind that give me a cold chill down my spine.

Time To Leave

January 17, 2001

San Quentin Prison has been getting more bad press. I heard on the news last night that the Q has way too many inmates housed to be safe. The feeling is that the prison should be torn down and rebuilt. A lot of lock downs have been going on inside the Q in the last few months because of gang riots.

After I sign in, I go inside and wait for my students. My aid tells me that a few years back, some friend of his family raped his sister's kid. She was only thirteen years old. He hunted down this guy and shot him in the head. He says he does not feel bad at all about shooting him. "He was a big fucking asshole. You don't screw around with little girls. It's just not right. So I played both judge and jury on that puke. Nobody messes around with my family and gets away with it. That asshole is dead and I'm locked away for the rest of my life. But that's okay! It was worth it just to see the look on his face before I blew him away. I'm not a monster; I'm just a loving, caring uncle who had to do what I had to do."

Right about this time inmates start showing up for the music class. The songs are "Free Bird" and the Johnny Cash song "Ring of Fire." Every inmate knows the words to "Free Bird" and believe it or not, the Indonesian inmate sings "Ring of Fire" without missing a word.

Around 8:45 p.m. I start to get a little tired, so I yawn, not thinking anything about it. My aid shouts at me, "Hey Buzzy! Don't start doing that shit around here. We all get up really early to go to work."

I ask him, "So what's early in prison? What time is wake-up call?" "4:30 a.m.," he tells me. "Some of us have jobs to go to. The pay is okay; but the commute is a real killer." At this point every inmate starts laughing. Prison jokes!

January 31, 2001

As I drive into the east gate I see one of the teachers I work with in the Juvenile Hall standing in line waiting to be cleared to go inside. I ask him how long he has been coming into the prison, and is he teaching a class here? He says, "I teach a Bible study class with some of the lifers through our church. We come to San Quentin once a month. I have been coming in here for about a year now. Have a good night."

When I start to sign in, I realize I have forgotten my prison whistle back at my house. I have to tell the officer on duty the truth. "There is no whistle; I left it at home." His reply to me is, "There's no way you're getting in here without a whistle and I don't have one to loan you for tonight." Right about this time, one of the prison church staff is coming into the Q. He says the church always has a couple of extra whistles locked up just in case someone like me forgets to bring theirs from home. He says, "I'll go and get a whistle for you to use tonight. Just return it when you leave. I'll be right back. Don't go anywhere; stay right here. Don't leave!" Watching the clock, I see twenty-five minutes crawl by. When he finally returns with the whistle, the officer on duty tells me I'm cleared to go inside the prison. When the man from the church and I enter the prison's courtyard together he turns to me and says, "You can give me the whistle back now, you won't need it. What can happen? Don't worry about it so much. You bring music to these inmates. They love you. You're not going to get hurt and besides I can't find the whistles; so can I please have that one back? It's mine."

I don't know what to do. I always say that I want adventure in my life, but this is asking for trouble. I have never been inside the prison without my whistle in three years of teaching music at the Q ever, except for tonight. I have always felt protected with that little whistle. But now that it's not here to blow if I need it, that makes me a tad nervous. What that man from the church said to me is true though. What can happen to me in prison? Students in music class love and respect the fact that I am coming into the prison to teach them. I'm not going to get hassled by anyone. To hell with it. I hand him back his whistle, and walk over to my classroom.

As I get closer, I notice that the door is open. When I walk into the room, I am greeted by my aid and ten inmates. My aid tells me everyone had gotten really worried about me; so he opened the room and just waited for me to get there. While I'm unpacking my guitar, I hear this inmate say, "Hey, Buzzy Martin. How have you been doing? Are you and Marco still playing music together? Are you still living in the same house in the same town? How are your wife and son doing?" This guy knows way too much about me for my safety. I stand straight up and without saying one word back, I start strumming my guitar. The more that I think about what has just happened, the more it creeps me out.

This inmate knows a lot about me and I have never seen him before in my life. The key word is the name Marco. He must know my good friend, Marco, because he knows about me. By now I'm starting to flip out inside. I become hot then cold and I feel like I am going to pass out. My heart is beating faster with every thought of this inmate's big mouth. I feel like I have just been bitten by a very mean dog. Every inmate in this class now knows where I live, my kid's name, where I work and what kind of truck I drive. This is not good. I can tell that a few inmates know something is very wrong because I just shut up. My face has turned white and I sit down.

In the meantime, I have eleven inmates ready to rock n' roll. For the next two hours, time drags on really slowly. By the time nine o'clock arrives, I am a wreck. All I can think about is why is this inmate asking me all these questions?

As class ends I look over at him. He looks a little like Charles Manson. He is short, dirty, and crusty looking. As he is walking out of the room, I ask him his name and prison number. To my shock and dismay, he is not even on my prison movement sheet. I tell my aid how concerned I am about this inmate's big mouth and how much it bothers me that he had slipped into music class so easily. I say that he knows way too much about my family. My aid tells me, "I saw red flags waving yesterday when he told me he knew you and some of your friends. I didn't know that he was such a big mouth. If you don't want him in the class, tell me and he's gone, boss. Just like that. You tell me what you want done." I tell him I have to call my boss and ask her what I should do about Mr. Big Mouth and what has happened. As I am talking to my aid, it hits me right between the eyes. My gig at San Quentin prison is over. I no longer feel safe working in the Q. I did not plan it, but the time has come for me to stop.

I pack up my guitar knowing that this is my last time walking the grounds of the prison. The last three years and five months have been the wildest, strangest and creepiest ride I can think of. But now it's all over, because of one big-mouthed inmate.

As I drive out of the prison parking lot, I take one last look at the Q and say goodbye. Driving home, I can't dial my cell phone fast enough. The first person I call is my wife, then my friend, Marco. I want to find out about this inmate that just blew away the music class with his big mouth.

My wife flips out. She starts crying right away. I tell her not to worry; it's over; I'm done. When I reach Marco on the phone, he tells me he is the one who called the police and had this inmate put back in prison. About six months ago, a neighbor of his started yelling, "Help me. He's hitting me. Help! He's going to kill me." So he called 911. When the police showed up this guy started fighting with the police officers. He was high on crack. He and his girlfriend had been drinking and smoking crack for days. He was arrested for parole violation, assault on an officer, narcotics, and was still on probation from his last string of crimes.

I ask Marco, "Do I have anything to worry about with Mr. Big Mouth?" There is a long pause. I say, "Hey, Marco, are you still with me?" In a real soft voice, he says, "I wouldn't trust him. He's kind of a weasel in a lot of ways. I wouldn't put anything past him. He's a nut."

That is it. That is my answer. I'm calling my Boss in the morning. I know what has to be done. I will quit tomorrow. "Good night, Marco. I will call you back after I talk to my boss."

     ·

I never thought I would end my music program at the prison in this way. I imagined maybe a riot or being caught in a lock down and held captive by some wild inmates, but not this — being freaked out over some big-mouthed inmate I do not even know.

By 8:00 a.m. the next morning my phone was ringing off the hook. My boss was calling to ask me about what happened last night in music class. My aid had already told her the whole story. She asked me how I felt and would I like to take a few weeks off to think about things? I told her yes. I need to think this thing over. I told her, "Give me two weeks." Those two weeks came and went. When I finally phoned my boss, she told me that some of the other inmates had beaten up the big-mouthed inmate because I had stopped coming into the prison to do music with them.

Well, that was it. My boss, her superior, and I all felt like the party was over. They both wished me well. Just like that. Three years and five months, over. I loved that class. I am going to miss a lot of those inmates but I felt like I was not safe anymore, so it was best to stop while I could just walk away from it. The pictures of San Quentin Prison and the inmates are burned in my mind for the rest of my life. I will never forget my time at the Ranch, H-Unit, and North Block. I will never forget the privilege of being able to work inside a prison for that long. How blessed and grateful I am to know the taste of freedom. What I have learned from this experience is the value of freedom.

Looking Back: What I Have Learned and What I Want To Tell You

January 31, 2001 was my last night at the Q. I was always reminded by my supervisors that familiarity is not a good thing in prison. That is the rule. It was time to go. I walked away from teaching the music program at San Quentin Prison without ever saying goodbye to anyone. I always told myself that if I ever felt uncomfortable about working in the prison, I would stop coming in and I did.

As this story came to an end, I turned yet another page of my life. I wondered what lay ahead in the future.

I hope and pray for a better world, more peace, less crime. It is a small world that we live in. I hope that some of you reading this book will help change it, even if it is just a little bit at a time. As for the kids who I have been working with in Juvenile Hall for the last eight years, some have gone on to have great lives, while others ended up becoming inmates at San Quentin Prison. I'm grateful that the music program helped even a few of them. Each life is precious. I'm still working with kids in the Hall. Unfortunately, the gang presence among younger kids is escalating with more violence. I'm also seeing a lot more Mexican and Asian gang members as young as twelve years old.

The stories floating around Juvenile Hall are that some former inmates from San Quentin Prison are recruiting kids from the streets to become gang bangers. Most have shaved heads, wear baggy pants, and are getting more violent. Young people in poor neighborhoods are short of hope.

Some of these kids come from single parent families; others from families of gang members. The strain on the justice system is overwhelming, to say the least. In the last three years, I have seen twenty young gang bangers end up getting life with no possibility of parole.

It hurts my soul to watch these young boys make bad choices in their lives. But through the music program and other programs like it, kids learn several powerful lessons: (1) They learn that music can help them express their emotions in productive ways, rather than through street violence and gang affiliation. (2) They experience a sense of accomplishment through hands-on basic instrument sessions. (3) They learn pride in the music traditions of their cultures. These are important lessons for these troubled, hard-to-reach youths. The goal of the program is not to produce professional musicians. The goal is to produce kids with improved self-esteem and social skills.

Music offers an effective way to reach people because humans are inherently musical. However, low self-esteem, violent behavioral patterns, or poor social skills prevent some kids and adults from expressing themselves. Singing, playing an instrument, dancing, and even listening to music for enjoyment are foreign to most of them.

A lot of kids' minds have been poisoned by the violent lyrics of gangster rap. The music program is about so much more than simply music. It's a unique therapy to improve self-esteem and provide an experience of success. Through music people can and do learn how to relate to each other. Playing music teaches discipline and focused practicing results in personal accomplishment.

The magic of music and this program puts them in touch with the power of creation, to which most of them have never been exposed. More programs like these are needed.

I am very glad to have had the chance to teach a music class at San Quentin Prison so I can share these stories with people who might open their hearts in some way. I would not change those three years and five months of my life for anything. I am still playing music with the band but life goes a little slower for me nowadays. I smell the flowers more. I kiss my wife and son a lot more.

I thank my wife and son for putting up with long nights when I was teaching at the Q. But most of all I want to thank you for taking the time to read this book. Perhaps there is something you can do to see that music is available to people who need it the most. We can make this planet a much better place for all of us by keeping music programs alive for all kids. It starts with the child inside all of us. Share a song with someone every day. May God bless you.

Buzzy Martin

Behind the Walls of San Quentin Prison

It's your first night in the Q and your cellmate
makes unwanted sexual advances toward you.

What would you do?

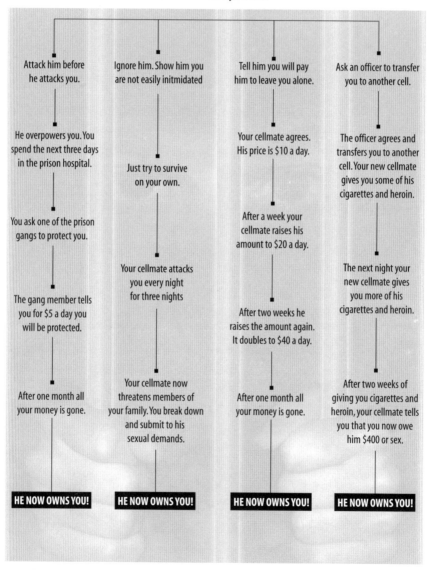

Attack him before he attacks you.	Ignore him. Show him you are not easily initmidated	Tell him you will pay him to leave you alone.	Ask an officer to transfer you to another cell.
He overpowers you. You spend the next three days in the prison hospital.		Your cellmate agrees. His price is $10 a day.	The officer agrees and transfers you to another cell. Your new cellmate gives you some of his cigarettes and heroin.
	Just try to survive on your own.		
You ask one of the prison gangs to protect you.		After a week your cellmate raises his amount to $20 a day.	
	Your cellmate attacks you every night for three nights		The next night your new cellmate gives you more of his cigarettes and heroin.
The gang member tells you for $5 a day you will be protected.		After two weeks he raises the amount again. It doubles to $40 a day.	
After one month all your money is gone.	Your cellmate now threatens members of your family. You break down and submit to his sexual demands.	After one month all your money is gone.	After two weeks of giving you cigarettes and heroin, your cellmate tells you that you now owe him $400 or sex.
HE NOW OWNS YOU!	**HE NOW OWNS YOU!**	**HE NOW OWNS YOU!**	**HE NOW OWNS YOU!**

Photo by Ellen Hanson Harris

Buzzy Martin was born and raised in Grand Rapids, Michigan. He is a professional musician, child advocate, and now an author. He resides in northern California.

To purchase this book contact:

Buzzy Martin
P.O. Box 2048
Sebastopol, CA 95473
e-mail: buzzymartin@sbcglobal.net
www.buzzymartin.com